Boro S

HISTORY AS A DICTATORSHIP OF CAPITAL

NEW YORK

2020

Boro Stipanovic

HISTORY AS A
DICTATORSHIP
OF CAPITAL

It belongs neither to gods nor to men by birth. Freedom is and will always be a universal endless process of constant development of human creative work, which enables the gradual emergence of a fundamental understanding of the universal movement in time and space, in the constantly new human psyche produced by creative work

NEW YORK 2020

Understanding the universe is only part-ly available to modern humanity. The millennia of the evolutionary presence of humanity in the universe compared to the speed of light that characterizes the universal duration are just a glimpse of the far greater process and self-creation that lies ahead of the future of human creative work, with which we can come significantly closer to understanding the infinite universe.

The primary and natural evolutionary characteristics of living beings are primarily defined by the natural imma-nent dictate of the life instinct different in each species and of almost innumerable qualities, which basically springs from the constant universal motion of various properties of matter and is as such woven into universal, particular and singular shapes and forms of constant motion and activities of both living and all other beings and objects in the universal infinity and process. With these primary properties of motion contained in our matter that belongs to us because we are part of the permanent motion of a far more extensive, richer and infinite material property of the universe, living beings are ensured continuous fundamental activity and efforts to ensure and protect, above all, the very activity of species survival as well as other activities that enable the movement of one's own matter, its reproduction (biological and self-creative formation), the right of "reasonable domination" over other beings and objects in the infinity of rational and irrational activities in which we consciously or unconsciously participate.

The main companion of all processes is constant quantitative and qualitative change. In living beings, apart from death, as a transition of some elementary property of matter into another evolutionary material property in a constant universal process, there are instinctive and instinctively defined activity and growing parallel conscious creative and self-creative activity which is constantly a new part of evolutionarily revolutionary and creative matter, primarily recognizable in the human being, but also visible in other biological and fellow beings. It seems, however, that most living beings still move on Planet Earth directed by the invisible forces of the universal motion of matter that defines and dictates all forms of primary instinct, but much more than that, its biological-evolutionary presence in constant motion.

In all living beings and at all stages of development, the mass instinct of survival and the instinct of reproduction predominate in a relatively primitive psychophysical consciousness that somewhat understands the closer horizons of the universal abode, while experiencing the rest of the universe horizon as an unknown and mystical landscape. It is only the transition from primary nervous to psych nervous activity within the universal movement that is typical of those living beings that possess specific properties of their own matter after gradually going through a series of complex evolutionary processes in which developing within their matter and its movement the ability for higher degrees of psychophysical creative work and self-creation by gradual creative work gave rise to a creative psychophysical consciousness of countless predispositions. At least for now, it has not been confirmed whether psychophysical highly organized matter created by the evolution of living beings or some other path that in its highest stage of development belongs to human beings, is the only psychophysical matter that consciously creates thought or whether there are other sets of independent both living and non-living suitable material or immaterial organization which also have the ability of rational, mental and psychophysical action in the universe. One thing is certain, at least for now, that mental and rational behavior is evident exclusively in living evolutionary beings where it gradually works, develops, records or arises in human creative and self-creative activity which always promotes psychophysical and rational features into higher and more complex forms of activity. Psychophysical beings, although still in evolutionary properties, are by their creative work and creation in transitional stages into revolutionary rational beings who, aware of compatibility with the universe or not, can significantly influence their compatible place and activity in its immediate processes. The impact and interventions of the psychophysical activity of the human species on the universe if they do not have compatible properties can have catastrophic consequences for the human species and its universal duration. The rationality of the universe is our everyday role model that we strive for with our creative work.

It is not known whether ideas and sets of ideas are free-floating collective evolutionary concepts immanent to universal motion until one incarnates them with one's own matter when one flashes one's presence to a conscious host. In human collective history, at least for the time being, they appear exclusively as part of our creative and self-creative work and process, everything else is not a reliable source of their presence or their origin or place of residence.

Herbivores, carnivores, insects, viruses, fish, bacteria, plants, birds, mollusks, mammals and all other beings, of course also people who, thanks to their rich creative, active and evolutionary salinity and conscious creative and self-creative history, are basically and in main features elementary conditioned by the universal movement. Creative human work springs from the same universal evolution of movement with which we have somewhat deviated from the cliché of basic evolutionary features of instinctive behavior, but not very far from other evolutionary companions, at least not seen in modern top features of creative production and the use of means to insure reproductive values of the social communities in which we live under the pressure of the rights of the stronger in modern forms of capital and capital relations. Despite the tenacious resistance to the primary instinctual evolutionary characteristics provided by modern humanity through creative and self-creative activity, the supernatural rudimentary instinctive animal force of unbridled instincts of greed, ruthless appropriation and control of conditions and means by which the stronger rule over the weak throughout history on the Planet Earth, it is much more deeply present in modern civilizational and universal achievements, which we often forge in stellar achievements in the modern history of civilizational cultures, than it is usually believed and accepted. From its primordial and most primitive forms of conscious creation and self-creation, humanity has constantly developed and created and still does, by exclusively more perfect means with which the stronger parts of humanity, individuals or groups that possess these means in strictly protected social relations, regularly and ruthlessly realize their advantage over the rest of the subjugated and weaker unprotected humanity. In such history and such human activity, humanistic features become the world of ideas, unattainable illusions on the distant horizon for most of the participants who are born and who perish.

It seems that the formed consciousness and general psychophysical activities during evolutionary creative and self-creative processes in the human species have enormously multiplied the present energy of uncontrollable instinctive forms of behavior which was gradually transformed into a rational creation of a means of necessary domination and survival and apologetics of the decomposition of all that is an obstacle to the domination of the psychophysical nature of the stronger on the way to the goal both within its biological species and the rest of living and material nature in its immanent universal movement. It is predicted in scientific and futuristic circles that such selfish and reckless irrational human behavior could lead human civilization to self-destruction. The means by which this advantage of a small number of people over the majority is realized in modern human society are sets of values and tools created by human creative work that exceed the basic needs of creative work and survival, which, throughout history as free values, we use and redirect in social relations for creation and formation of new conditions for the realization of our work and the work of other people in a new accumulation and the formation of new free capital in our favor.

There has always been another's labor as a means that a human being can use as well as the human labor market for all those who have not acquired in human history a sufficient amount of free surplus value and means to subdue, buy and acquire the value of another's labor for their gain and action, but also for those who possessed surplus accumulations from other people's wage earners past work and who maintained both the labor market and the wage population of human history. Also, work that produces new value in human history could always be legally used, bought or paid compensation to useful profit in both primary groups and secondary groups, primarily the family, which as a primary group had a number of complex emotionally rational production functions so that its original features are still used as a model in the jargon of everyday business and marketing language "we are all a family of brothers and sisters", as a foundation of functional and creative characteristics of human groups. The work of women, mothers and sisters, and their historical position in all stages of social development has almost regularly been subordinated to the biologically stronger male sex. These primary characteristics of the position of the female sex within the modern family are still manifested today in the position of women in modern human communities and modern families. Literally half of humanity (female) has always been subordinated in all its creative and self-creative functions to the dominant male sex who mastered wage labor and their loved ones in the primary groups. This gender relationship has not changed significantly today because the position of the family in the most developed societies in its basic standards of survival and functions has not changed, even the traditional family is disappearing and whatever new form and practically formed creation inherits has a primary wage earners character again, conditioned by capital and capital relation as it was in the traditional family. Mothers are still unreasonable victims of reckless and selfish dominant (mostly male) owners of capital and legal jurisdictional and moral criteria with which social communities are modeled, although their work and reproductive social and family functions should be marked with far different respect and reward than what is the case today in the most developed communities of the world.

The method of payment for wage labor in the labor market that creates new values, which partly includes the free value of previous past human labor in order to multiply under given legal conditions, is primarily provided from part of the wage labor or anticipated planned wage earners use by the owner of money (capital) that buys it, which is realized in a new value and divides by the price of wages and the wage unpaid to the earner appropriated by the owner of the money invested in the reproduction procedure. It is this value that the wage earner has created but does not belong to him that creates the accumulation of new free capital which is recorded in favor of the owner who organizes and re-invests new and greater free values in the social relation of production in order to make even greater earnings for his private benefit, or the benefit of the corporation owned or co-owned by him. When the owner of capital pays social functions from this part of his and corporate money, there is always a function of social organization (as well as wage earnings) in his mind, which is only a means of his earnings and his profits. During the historical development, in the minds of the owners of capital, the essential feature of the social communities of organized wage earners has usually been only a means to achieve their own goals. Anyone who has ever been recognized in human history as an investor in human labor and who has legally employed and used the work he paid at the agreed price knows very well that he has gained significantly more than the work and compensation to the wage earner, otherwise the work that hires wage earners would have no meaning for the owner of the capital nor would it ever be realized as the value of past labor in the form of possession of material goods or free capital (money) invested by the investor in that process. Of course, in no phase of the historical development of entrepreneurship did the possessors of the capital created by the past work of wage earners have any intention or obligation, either under legal secular or divine laws, to express this newly created free value as a result of wage labor or to let their wage earners know how much new value they made for the owner of the capital in addition to the portion of the known value paid in wages. Thus, a legal millennial diversion was created for all participants in history, in which the recording of the value of someone else's wage labor, both in quality and quantity, is always done in favor of the owner of capital.

The revolution of all freedom is a state of human creative practice and a natural relation to the universe which is our natural evolutionary source. The revolution of freedom and free creation disappeared in parallel from the perspective of wage labor, and also the freedom of all other beings and participants that are directly or indirectly controlled by "free" dominant capital and its few owners who also become unconditional masters of human creative work in a legally created social relationship without which its creation and realization is impossible. The free and unspent value of the past work of wage earners regularly owned by the employer in the form of capital, reinvested in wage labor anywhere and anytime throughout history and even today is the only source of accumulation of new free value (capital) for each subsequent reproduction and human creation. This is also the cause of the geometric progression of capital and profit growth, but also of the political legal and economic power and possessions of the owners of the formed capital arising from the historical currents of the past work of the wage earners of the world. This process continues today. A free independent set of values integrated in the psychophysical unity of individuals, in their formal and legal possession or the possession of a group of owners, institutions, banks, corporations, states and other entities that has countless alternatives to redirect multiplication and increase exclusively through creative and controlled of human labor we call capital. Capital is the private possession of the value of past live current labor. Capital is the possession of a larger or smaller group of values or the possession and control of the pragmatic growth of all values (not just monetary value) that everyone possesses, controlled by dominant capital that defines total social reproduction both locally and globally. The capital that we recognize in our closest peculiarities is primarily the value of our wage earning and socialized personal psychophysical unity, which we form through creative and self-creative work. Capital is both a creative anticipation and a dream and reality in the image and motives of our consciousness of its significance that we are obsessed with and without which we cannot function.... In the reality of capital, in addition to being formed in earlier processes of creation and self-creation and presented by appropriate measuring instruments, it appears in our personality as a possession and process of self-awareness of one's own values of material or any other property in social relations. Capital, in its broadest character, is the possession of all the values that serve and guarantee the next, especially expanded, reproductive capital relation in which we participate. With measured quantified and qualified characteristics that we are familiar with rationally or in some other way, we constantly compare ourselves with other human beings or members of other communities, different capital relations, and in these relations we are always aware of creative and self-creating values and potential of other people's work which we would like to possess. Measurements and observations of other people's work and values regularly direct us to the possible possession of the value of other people's work or possession of creative and self-creative predispositions of other creators and self-creators that can be legally managed as planned value in creation and self-creation in future reproductive periods. Possessing and controlling both past labor as capital and also current labor ensures the infinite possession of power in a social relationship. Capital, which is the fruit of human labor itself, cannot exist without a social relationship and pragmatic social value systems of human past and current labor that are measurable and that are constantly controlled in that measurable and quantitative and qualitative relationship.

These realized planned and quantified and qualified values of capital through and after the reproductive cycles of past and current work are appropriated through legal dictate which is an imperative obligation of conduct for all, marked within legal systems that are also an integral part of free unspent capital that produces and creates new values, which is primarily a part of private capital in the possession of naturally wealthier, richer, privileged, and stronger legal subjects in social relations who create them and dictate them according to their own need. Having legal systems and being able to create and supplement them on a daily basis as part of OWN procedural CAPITAL that directs social forces or free values that we can change and supplement according to the needs imposed by the pragmatics of successful reproductive cycles is another important feature of legal dictatorship of capital accumulation in the possession of a small number of owners whom we recognize as the dictators of capital over creative human labor of all kinds. No matter how creative and skilled a person is, without an appropriate legal system that defines social rules of capital relations (or some form of common law), they will not be able to realize or appropriate significant sums of surplus value or form capital exclusively for their own benefit. In addition to human creative work in material production, the creation of free capital or accumulation requires the production of social relations and a legal system that is dictated by the legalization of such practices and the exploitation of all use values, both natural and man-made. This dictate through the possession of the legal system as part of free capital is a necessary condition that defines the exploitation of creative human labor of those members of society who are in no way in possession of free capital, except that, by social capital relation, they are dependent owners of their working and creative being that they offer in the reproductive cycle in the form of capital, which we most often present as the value and price of an hour of work or work on quantitative characteristics of one day, month or year of work and other characteristics. Hence the title of wage-earning population of the world for that most numerous stratums of humanity. It is precisely these engaged layers of wage earners in historical and contemporary streams of reproduction that by their creative and self-creative work create primarily themselves, new use values but also the fundament of those values that ensure adequate accumulation of free new private capital always intended for new social reproduction over which it dominates. Through their work, new values created by labor for all participants in reproductive relations are made aware of and socially announced.

The overall social relationship is constantly under the control of the owner of capital and his subjugated political and managerial partners through the legal economic and political system as always a new legal social relationship which is also in further productive social relations constantly supplemented and exploited for the benefit of those who create it. All political parties and all legal, political and economic systems throughout history have essentially and primarily originated and are still emerging and are formed to permanently ensure the accumulation and capital of past and current work of wage earners which will form both future operating capital and defined practice of capital relations in favor of the creators of those systems as an integral part of that capital. Legal political and economic systems, together with private owners of accumulation and capital, in the existing history and modernity are regularly conditioned servants of a given accumulation and dictates of the future survival of dominant capital, which, with growth, also becomes an independent supernatural dominant force that governs the behavior and basic characteristics of our socializations. The socio-political systems that ensure accumulation are essentially capital in possession and a tool of capital of both past and live current labor. Likewise, new political legal and economic systems, without the means to create, are created to demolish and destroy old or parallel forms of accumulation that are on the way to dominant more pragmatic and stronger capital around the world: there is no mercy in the dictates of capital. In these procedures, even the most extreme means of destruction are used, regardless of the victims, in order to achieve the goals and alliances. The stativity of accumulated capital regularly ends in losses in all political, legal, and economic systems of the world, about which the past history of mankind abundantly argues modern science and our current socializations that shape us. The process of awareness in circumstances that allow embraced advantages of legal exploitation of society relations creates real pragmatic forms of capital existence and capital relations, but also scientific and idolatrous apologetic notion in our consciousness of that reality and applicative anticipation of its possible universal values which, with time and abundance of human creative work, gradually form into a comprehensive qualitative and universal worldview. For now, humanity does not know different, more dominant, and experienced forms of social relations that the history of human creative creation has achieved. Universal values of legal exploitation of human labor and exploitation of other values in nature and the universe, as well as the accumulation of capital are absolutely dominant social relations of history and present. It seems that we could state that in the political-economic equation: Capital = Variable Capital (wage earners)/Constant Capital (means of productions) x working time, which is as old as homo sapiens, we can find almost all our basic characteristics and definitions. And all the particular emergent and parallel forms and systems of political and social transformation that this universal principle gave birth to in past human history, whose goal was to change this existing universal feature of change, did not have enough strength and argumentation to be accepted in new processes of social realities nor have these new systems made significant changes in their practice even when the violent means of some other different dictatorships were used. All earlier generations in our evolutionary genesis have accepted, despite the resistance of smaller sections of the human population, the exploitation of other people's labor and the creation of an accumulation as a common process that can not only be legalized into a legal economic, political, cultural, philosophical, scientific, religious or even ethical system of any part of our everyday life as a system accepted by "all" living participants in social communities of any stratum of the past and present historical reality, but also as a vision of the legal future and the position and role of human creative and self-creative work of all wage earners who provide significant foundations of all existing and future values. Such human history, and we do not know another, has created rational egoism as a practice, different though partly based on the instinctive egoism of the elementary evolutionary nature of living beings as its logical sequence which we encounter in the dissected anatomy of modern world societies in its original animal form, as well as in all layers of political legal and economic systems created by the modern wage earner protagonist, the rational creator and self-creator of new useful human values.

Everyday legality of historical reality is in fact the general state of the legal system that we create and use ourselves and with which we participate daily in our communities as wage earners or as wage earners who own capital with the aim of creating new accumulation and new capital.

Word "Legalis" is coming from Latin language that was in us in Rome. Meaning of the word is adherence to precise law. It is no wonder that even today in the existing systems we feel limited and defined within the legal regulations that bind us and oblige us. This attachment or determination for each individual within the social communities that nurture capital relationship was a well-known feature of wage earners from the beginning of wage labor and the Romans defined it by the Latin term legatus which means to bind (give it a function in practice) within the hierarchy of dominant values, that is, capital and capital relations.

Thus, for Western civilization and under its influence and its jurisdictional sciences, an essential feature of all social systems of the world is summarized in a perfect term and other related terminology.

Legality and the legal system is not complete and does not belong to the moral principled solutions, although its creators, authors and the most frequent users want to present it as a moral principled solution, which especially refers to the basic constitutional laws that are essential and most legal and, due to their unfinished and incomplete achievements, require the largest and most extensive expert arbitration and relentless changes that are reluctantly made. We are constantly witnessing processes in which the legality and laws of everyday life are in constant process of enlargements by the arbitration of an authority that interprets laws. In modern societies, the legality of adopted laws that live in practice if they are in part or in full disputed, is completed in arbitral legal hearings of supreme courts, which complete and establish the pragmatics of the applicability of law. Arbitration experts may have different political views and interests, but in existing systems they are primarily in the realm of pragmatic legality rather than the general ethical values of universal significance and openness. Everything is like one of the versions of the saying "the judge sues you, the judge judges you" in which nothing moves if there is no pragmatic capital gain at its core. Complete legal systems or laws completed and ethically defined as principled morality do not exist in practice. What has formed legal practice throughout history is primarily private ownership of mass creative wage labor and the values of their production of new values in the entire production of all necessary use values and the creation of accumulation and capital, but also the constant creation and improvement of a pragmatic profile which we recognize in the legal political and economic system. Legality in modern societies is quite ambitious but at the same time dispersive and marked by the hyperproduction of laws of extensive usability, mostly up-to-date and protective in relation to the protection of the dominant pragmatic practice of wage production of private property, accumulation, capital and capital relations. However, its greatest legal value is based on the productive creative and self-creative work of wage earners, which enables constant changes and fluidity of political legal and economic systems, that is, new legality and new practice. Most of the changes expected in the future in the legality of conventional legal systems will occur due to the accelerated growth of creative wage labor, which with its increasing quantitative and qualitative function and presence in reproductive systems of creation of new use values will suppress exclusively private ownership of accumulation and capital. The new non-ownership rights to use part of the accumulation and capital in the initial stages of future socio-economic reproductions will emphasize the growing need for creative wage labor to belong to its accumulation and its capital, and less and less to private equity. Hybrid social relations of such characteristics can be seen even today. Today's legal systems do not have to accept scientific arbitration or an explanation with which to be instructed in changes that do not belong to the dominant practice of creating accumulation and capital. The supreme arbitrage of legality is still only a legal supplement that needs arbitration again, and if it is not possible or based on legal proceedings, it is certainly not excluded from the temporal arbitration that arises in parallel with the growth of wage creative work of future communities. Modern legal systems are still able to delay the answer to a number of open questions, especially those found in the theoretical and analytical models of political economy and other social sciences and humanities, due to the flow and dominant features of modern legality. Avoiding and postponing the scientific truth about the exploitation of wage labor on behalf of capital and its owners over the course of history will certainly gain its final qualitative qualification in the same way that slave-owning society and slave labor and the legality of these social systems at least in their classical form got it in the US civil war, but also much earlier in other historical places and divisions of human history. It is a matter of time and growth of the creative and self-creative work of wage earners, which will create both awareness and the need to definitely decide in the future on the fate of slavery of all wage earners and the human community to capital and the capital relation.

Private ownership legality and the right to exploit the human wage labor of contemporary historical practice is, as we have already emphasized, the dominant form of reproduction of the modern world. The historical human being wants to be "I" with the right to possess the value of both his own and other people's work of past and live current work... Still, even in the deepest intimacy, no human being wants to be "WE". The identification of individuals with society (which enables them) has never throughout history been the dominant goal or motive of human creative work and creation. "I" ..., is a well-known and close value that integrates contemporary reality and visions of universal value into individual possession, enabled by the integration of own and others' work into private possession of accumulation and capital, while "WE" is in the existing state of consciousness and with existing creative means a rather dispersive and distant motive and landmark of humanity unrealistic to be the primary motive for everyone.

In our everyday reality and socialization, when we notice that the "I" possesses the universal, the particular, and the singular, we immediately identify with it, but if "WE" acquires these attributes or practices, it becomes the cause of the misfortune of our singular superior arrogant individual historical being. The disappearance of our "I" and its painless rational transformation into a functional, rational and more efficient historical means that we call "WE" in this context is a process that began in earlier history but in order for it to be fully realized in the actual everyday process, its dominance in relation to contemporary historical reality, it requires far better and more quantitative results of human creative and self-creative work than what today's human creation demonstrates.

The "I" as we know it today as our own creative and self-creating consciousness and practice would never have been possible without the exploitation of wage earners ("We"), other people's work and other values, and the creation of accumulation and free capital in private ownership. Of course it is impossible to answer the question of what our history would be or what our future would be without wage labor in favor of the accumulation and capital of a few private owners, until we are familiar with more efficient creative and self-creative processes that will shape the procedures and processes of independence and compatible rational universal creativity and wage creativity that is superior to the rational capitalist egoism and wage exploitation of today, which, as our daily practice, we achieve in the capitalist and socialist communities of the world that use the accumulation derived from the exploitation of other people's labor, capital and capital relation. However, in order to complete part of my thoughts, at least in the process, I must state that any solution that suddenly turns its back to the whole of the past of we possess and the only history we possess using radical revolutionary forms of change is hopeless. The grandiose layers of historical institutions (although partly completely useless) in which we still reach our maximum reach are an essential foundation but also a limitation of creative and self-creative work and our practice on which our future depends. And as such, they will be our future companions for a long period to come.

For many generations of wage earners, this inconceivable process of change that many wanted but did not experience, is equally present today for modern creative wage earners in the world. Even today, this process is slow and limited by capital pragmatics, the form of wage creation and self-creation that has its endless models conceived in earlier history, which are visible in the vague futuristic visions of the world of the future present among us today. Both before and today, these models are divided and can be placed in two basic recognizable profiles: a) accumulation, capital and profit belong in their genesis to the wage earners of the world and in the future they are destined to be rational managers of human creative and self-creative work and will, in accordance with their new developing functions which must be much more efficient than existing functions provided by capital and capital relation, gradually achieve a new legal economic and political system of the future b) accumulation, capital and profit will continue to belong to smaller groups of owners of accumulation and capital to their legal and political systems and institutions that we have known for a long time throughout history with gradually adopted changes that will generate creative human work. Neither solution, at least not in its primary fundamental functional and temporal orientations, will be possible without respecting the basic principles of the survival of capital and capital relations as the basic pragmatic instrument of our immediate future. The questions of who will have accumulation, capital and profit and what transformations are expected in this regard are a parallel pragmatic framework of all participants in creative work to which the future will pay far more attention in more rational democratic processes than before. Democratic processes in the future, which in addition to the new democratic

dynamics will have a rational creative dynamics of principled rather than legal tendencies, will always pay special
attention to the pragmatics of the purpose of total capital
or social wealth in the way of directing it primarily not to
the benefit of private property but of a rational public benefit purpose. The new accumulation and capital that will
enable this in its rational scope must be created by human
creative past work and expanded (increased compared to
the previous cycle) reproductive creative processes of live
current work. Pragmatic logic of visions and horizons of
human creative work and the most democratic society of
the future completely and again as in the previous history
depend on the newly created use value of both producers of means of production and production of means of
consumption, with the highest technical and technological achievements and accumulation of capital and joint
profit which will be recorded as a result and potential of
future creative work of all layers of wage earning social
communities. The principal drivers and implementers of
social reproductions will remain entirely the same as in
modern entrepreneurial capitalism. What the new rational
democratic stratifications of capitalism and new scientific,
technical and technological solutions and their penetration
into the reproductive currents of modern socio-economic
relations of capital and capital relations will bring is the
increasing availability of accumulation, new capital and
profit to creative wage protagonists of reproductive cycles.
The existence of ownership, whether social or private, over
accumulation, new capital and profit will not be possible
simply because all ownership relations over accumulation

and capital will have a principled rather than legal rational solution acceptable primarily as the right and duty of pragmatic creative work of all professions or all reproductive functions for the benefit of all mankind. Billionaire private property will be an administratively unnecessary absurdity in the future. With the gradual disappearance of private and social property, a new form of attitude towards the means of production and consumption and creative human labor (wage labor) will emerge. All participants in the reproductive process will have the right and duty of creative work and creation as an elementary human right. With the disappearance of private and social ownership, the privileged position of accumulation, new capital and profit of all alternatives that were known in earlier history and used as capital relations under the control of smaller ownership or bureaucratic groups of people will disappear. The typical, earlier, and present imperial history of capital, especially financial capital, will disappear over time. In addition, although the rational democratic future of creative creators in wage creative work will have the most important ally and creator, it is to be expected that the selection of wage creativity will be far more comprehensive, rational and pragmatic than it is today in private capitalism. The goal of this selection and choice of commitment is not only a new creative quality of human creation but also raising human creative work to the level of self-conscious managerial production and social functions that belong to it, which have been subordinated to private interests, capital and its owners for millennia. In the future awakening, raising, and equalizing both the quality and quantity of human creative work, in addition to the usual creative work through wage efforts, principled science will be the primary ally. According to modern research, the capacity of a wage earner when working for another as a hired worker is 15-20% less than when working for himself or general social and common interests, which also indicates long-term and unrecorded consequences of catastrophically harmful suppression of massive potentials of human creative work throughout history within the capital relation, regarding which no one is responsible or obligated in the legality of legal systems as they are today to record these events. Like it or not, modern legality and the practice of human communities are in their basic features' devastation and destruction of that kind.

The future will be far more immersed in radical and rational information technology, and every wage earner whom the future will call a pragmatic rational creator will be part of a general rational memory that will constantly inform him about his creative social functions and duties, just as he does to it in return, in order for him to be as useful to it as possible during his working and creative life. Permanent social creative and work functions and the results of his work will be an integral part of his personal and social public, available to all participants in future reproductive processes. His consumption will be defined primarily by the standard humanistic minimum available to all citizens as a necessary condition of their procedural creative and self-creative function and will be based on the values of the part of newly created value of his creative work that remains after alimenting and financing social needs from the same newly created value of his work. Rational joint creative commitments of entire communities will be compatible with individual and personal life commitments of individuals. Pathological individual greed, selfishness, recklessness, unbridled animal greed, devastating wars and strategies of defense and attack, lies and biased arbitrage should also disappear from human history in the future. The means by which humanity already achieves this in long-term processes of work and wage earners creation is creative human work and the gradual elimination of the legality of legal systems in order to maintain the principled scientific legal order and definition of the value of human creative work. Apart from creative and self-creative work, other means and tools are neither available to humanity now nor will they be in the future.

The modern economic elements that maintain the intensive production of capital in our social communities today and the relations of capital are neither eternal nor perfect, but that means even less that they will soon disappear from the historical scene. All participants in historical processes are constantly and arbitrarily taught uncritically that human creative and self-creative history is dictated by higher powers possessed by the sanctity of capital and capital relations in private property systems and that our civilization culture is unconditionally subordinated to that capital and its owners. Libraries of theories and worldviews are multiplied, arguing millennial capital relations that are arbitrarily interpreted by various pragmatic philosophies, arts, religions, apologetic sciences, literature, politics, legal systems, science, work culture, technology, university and earthly transport, communications, information and information systems, military sciences, and many other fields that shape us as submissive consumers of the idolatrous marketing of subordinate capital that we ourselves have created regardless of whether we are its real and formal owners, possessors, or just its wage earners.

Yet in this whole vortex of historical events there is an independent core and area of creative activity and movement that has never been and does not possess this fatal subordinate properties of slavery to the inviolable properties of capital, this independent area is a process of creative and self-creative human work, especially the sphere of material production, and all other forms of creation that form the sphere of the social values of capital and capital relations. Creative activity today, regardless of the fact that its result in wage earners labor ends in accumulation, capital and profit of private property is the general gospel, a ray of light that promotes us into the infinite reality of the universe as compatible university beings even when our creative work is controlled and constantly dominated by capital. We must certainly not forget the fact that it is regularly parallel to positive and compatible universal creativity and the creative work of negative reactionary tendencies, even more so it dominates the egoistic nature of the pragmatics of capital itself and the capital relations that fully defines us in all processes. The creative sphere of material production of all kinds, including the production, creation and self-creation of new lasting psychophysical features of human matter, enables primarily increasing understanding but also our general compatibility with the universe that essentially defines and enables us as part of its constant processes and universal movements. Wherever we turn, both in the reality around us and in the reality within us and in our metaphysical being that anticipates both our reality and our future, the properties of capital are all around us primarily as a driving personal or social dictated force. Without being taken into account, if at all possible and I don't think so, these capital values and properties of capital and capital relations primarily in their being formed in causal interaction with socially dominant capital values and our creative and self-creative work become unrecognizable and unusable in the processes of historical currents. It is in this formed reality of our being created in creative work that it is recognized that even the most perfect dominance of capital in its properties and strength, although it initiates our engagement and wage creation without which it cannot survive, has no permanent possibility to rule the essential act of our creative human work. The symbiosis of creative wage labor and capital increasingly defines creative current human labor as the dominant subject that transforms the accumulation of capital and capital itself into a dependent and less dominant factor of reproductive cycles. I believe that not only will there be a few points in the world that exist today as an example of top creativity like Silicone Valley, but that the future will bring permanent creativity to everyone's doorstep. The act of creation is the only form of increasingly dynamic emergence of human freedom that will then form a new quantitative quality and leave the dictatorship capital and capital relations of a small number of private owners and bureaucrats and change the existing apologetic legal system that exists solely to maintain the dictated function of capital and capital relations and their owners. It is the growth of the creative work of wage earners that will enable the growth and transformation of these same wage earners into a growing population of rational managers with realized values of their own work, accumulation and capital as a newly created common value. Gradually, new legal political and economic systems closer to the mass and organized creative creativity of the majority will emerge. Even today, the same intention is present within the nature of the dictates of capital, but with the goal of a particular non-universal accumulation of capital that is gradually decomposing. We must be aware, not even the act of creative work as we know it today, which faces a bright future, is at this point in human creative wage earners history capable of eliminating capital and the capital relation as the dominant tool of human historical reality. That is why human history has created and still creates and maintains the inevitable symbiosis of the violent dictatorship of capital and the creative and self-creative worker of humanity, which is the only expression of freedom that a human being actually possesses. These processes in which the dominance of the creative subject of human labor and not capital will be visible, will increasingly appear and develop as a mass phenomenon. We can already see them present in their rudimentary forms visible in everyday life

similar to evolutionary natural selection within quantitative and qualitative features of human species and nature
in general, in which the transition of general quantitative
values into a new more comprehensive quality dictated by
human creative work is inevitable, no matter who organizes it in production reproductive processes or displays
and appropriates it as capital or newly created social value. Figuratively speaking, it is inconceivable that human
creative and self-creative future will be eternally and violently defined by the will and usurpation of the general
legal, political and economic power of 1% (or a much
smaller number) of the population as it is today. In this
symbiosis of continuous and quantitative and qualitative growth of both capital and creative human work and
self-creation, all human beings are formed and disappear
from the historical scene, leaving behind a recorded shift
woven into the foundations of the future of capital and
creative new processes of human current work, which can
be shallow or of exceptional ranges and amplitudes of creation. In this way, for millennia, only one goal has been
achieved and recorded in human history, the accumulation of usable property of all kinds of capital dictated and
quantified and qualified values created by human creative
work in all strata appropriate to capital relations around
the world. Every human being who is conceived and after birth resides among other working and creative human
beings and with his subdued and conscious creative and
self-creative appearance to the world and among other beings brings new value with his current work. Likewise, he
disappears from the creative reality of this planet in the

characteristics of his own capital. Someone as "nobody and someone as a valuable and irreplaceable man who left a deep mark" remembered by generations... Both the first and second characteristics of people and their creative being are acquired and given in the socialization provided by communities that form us as part of a much wider of the dominant creative capital values and its reproductive cycles. All previously created values, even today's ones, which we recognize in the dominant trend of recognizable individualism of each person within each layer of social structure, significantly depend on the quantity and quality of accumulation of values of our own and other people's past creative work, which we adopt and which forms us as active and creative beings consciously determined by the new reproductive cycles of the immediate future in which we participate

DICTATORSHIP OF CAPITAL

The word dictatorship has its origin in Latin and in the etymological basis of the word itself but also in the social characteristics of the usable content of the word as a fundamental concept that is constantly evolving through creative practice from the original etymological basis of the term dice dicere lat., which means to say. This term is certainly one of the few terms that is in different languages parallel to human origin and the first rudimentary voices that had meaning and significance among primates. The term dictatorship and similar concepts of the same meaning, which we use today in various thought variations and expressions, originate primarily owe to a whole group of terms of common etymological and social character that we find in Latin for a word that has the meaning of expressing an important and clear revelation based on generally accepted values in the social relation created by human work and activity. In many linguistic theories, creative human work stands out as a condition for the emergence of any language. It could be concluded that work and human creative activity create language or a means of rational publication and communication with which we as social beings use in everyday creative and social life to enhance the social relationship of creating new values or as we usually say today in theories of capital accumulation from current human creative work. The language we communicate with is one of the most effective tools of human capital and appears as an understandable and acceptable value not only through our speech but as a written word and text or a universally recognizable sign of innumerable and quantitative and qualitative values with which we communicate in everyday processes of producing social values especially in new information systems and their accelerated pragmatic development. The properties of the language allow the use of all other creative means. Here are just some of these terms in Latin that we can find in all other languages under other voice tags: dicto, in Latin as the first person singular means I speak, I wright, I express my thought, dictus exponent, dicta - act of legal authority, dictate direct statement, dictate order...., or the interesting and indicative term dictator, which in Latin in Roman everyday life refers to the name for a judge with unlimited, undisturbed and absolute commanding power, which is closest in meaning to dictatorship, a term which in its significance and historical genesis are touched upon in this book. In Greek culture, which helped to form Roman culture as an example of its practice, the dictator is a tyrant - a person with unlimited power (the rule of a tyrant or tyranny is a very common form of power dictated by the nature of capital which we know essentially in its nature and cannot survive otherwise). Presidential systems of recent history dictated by capital belong to the same historical provenance and often, with their far richer practice, far surpass their Roman or historical models. Modern presidential functions in many countries of the world are most similar in content, scope and reach to the Roman dictator who is not only in the role of the judge we have already mentioned but also in the role of ruler formed and enabled by Roman democracy and the Roman Senate. Almost all legal presidential systems that we respect today and in which we live owe their basic characteristics and the emergence of independence to the historical derivation that follows from the primary functional Roman dictatorship and the task that dictatorship and dictator had, which is to preserve and increase the accumulation and capital of existing communities. The capital of Rome created the dictators of Rome just as American capital dictates the behavior of American presidents today. The almost unlimited power that is an integral part of the function of modern presidents of the capitalist presidential systems of the world basically defines them as an independent subject in their actions for two reasons a) protection of their position and programs and actions from the influence of mass democracy whose goal is the dysfunctional stratification and loss of dominant capital held by a small number of people, b) protection of successful capital and value systems but also capital and capital relations that we want to achieve in the present and future through defined and controlled reproduction procedures of production of society or the world. To illustrate this influence and the dictates of capital given to the ruler, leader or dictator in modern conditions, we can state more clearly that the dictates of British dominant capital in its unconditionality which is passed on to only one person, created the possibility for that person to form a decision in the role of British Prime Minister (Boris Johnson) to dissolve the British Parliament in 2019, although this is not in line with the legal system that anticipated such a possibility of British democratic reality. The richness of pragmatic modeling of usurped power by dictators who are necessarily representatives of dominant capital is at the same time resistance to static forms of traditional conduct of democratic bodies of parliamentary power that are usually slow and quite inefficient. Often the dynamics of democratic decisions are as important as the speed of capital circulation in reproductive cycles, and "democratic sacrifices" in the name of capital are inevitable, understandable, and tolerated at a given time. Dictators in Rome were initially elected to their positions only in crisis situations when the senate was forced to appoint the most capable person for a limited time, usually 6 months, to be the absolute master of Roman everyday life in order to resolve the crisis as soon as possible. The period of 6 months was later usurped, and many rulers of Rome appropriated the right to a permanent dictatorship unlimited in time. The whole of Rome was without question obliged to carry out the orders of the dictator in those 6 months or for a longer time. Acquiring the right of unconditional dictate which maintains and creates new value is, as we see, not only a linguistic imperative form but a primary feature of creative and self-creative dominant capital as it is at a given moment in history (crisis problem solving) which, in parallel in the dialectical processes of opposition, enables the emergence of language itself and its meaningful use. The process of language-capital relation has another face, language enables the existence of capital and capital relations, which we have already mentioned in describing and defining the necessary symbiosis of capital and creative work both in reality and in appropriate and parallel legal systems that are an integral part of capital and its fluid flow of creation and transformation into new accumulation and new increased capital and profit. Legal systems (Rule of Law) are, as we see, a linguistic dictate of capital, which is constantly and if necessary supplemented with new content. In addition to the term that refers to the dictatorship in Latin in developed Roman society, this "dictate" of reason or commanding absolutely undisturbed property elevated above human everyday life does not begin with either Greece or Rome, but is an originally known and parallel principle with the ancient primordial values of creative and self-creative work of human beings and created useful objects of human labor that form capital and dictate capital relations or forms of societies that will consume this usability throughout later history.

In addition to this well-known dictate of capital and the capital relations that has been present throughout human history as a primary social relationship, it is noticeable that we are less aware of the presence and susceptibility in us and around us to the primordial universal "dictate" of matter to which we belong as universal beings. Universal "dictate" is the first and primary and dictates the movement of all matter, while the second dictate, the dictate of capital, has a much narrower dominance, scope and reach and has no permanent feature in the universe and its order. Its dominance is achieved only over creative and self-creative work and newly created use values of human work, which are imperatively given to us through the capital relations. The first is the dictate that we call the universal eternal motion of matter which cannot be violently altered by a human or any other being residing in the vastness of the universe and known as a conscious creative and self-creating being. The second dictate, which is basically enabled by the first dictate in singular, particular and universal existence, can be changed and redirected in accordance with the gradual adoption of compatible laws of the first universal dictate through past work as memory of the culture of capital creation and creative current creative work that brings us closer to understanding and living in accordance with the primary dictates and universal laws which are the condition of our universal cosmopolitan freedom. Unfortunately, humanity is far from an essential understanding of universal laws, but also from the abolition and overgrowth of the dictates of capital as another important feature in its entire scope that defines the creative and self-creative developmental paths of the human being in the universe. Liberation from the restraint of capital is a continuous process which is at least partially realized by human creative and self-creative work. Complete liberation from the dictates of capital is not possible for now. In the current circumstances, liberation from the dictates of dominant capital occurs only through the death of individuals, groups, or the whole of humanity.

Roman everyday life is certainly for many a concise form of the most valuable achievements of history, but also the foundation of many parts of modern civilizational culture of the world. Roman dictator or authoritarian and absolute judge and ruler got his property and strength not only by decision of other senators and co-rulers, but also from daily practices and pragmatics made up of created, accessible and usable values of human creative and self-creative work which over time were refined and rationally formed into symbols of linguistic forms in "dictates", into commanding value statements, according to immanent properties of values from which legal systems known today as the "rule of law" were created. Legal systems are written and created in the language generated in creative and self-creative processes of current work and are intended to protect the process of creation and creative and self-creative values of human labor. With this written code we also define the social general status characteristics of capital in the consciousness of the human being and his psychophysical unity. The legal system defines each degree and value of human creative current work and its products as well as the turnover value of these products and the interaction of all other values in the social relationship that have their origins in human creative work. Dictate and features of dictate known to the Romans were not applicable in India at the time or vice versa, the specificity of Indian caste culture was not applicable in Rome. Likewise, modern social relations dictated by modern capital and capital relations have advanced considerably, both in their creative abundance and in general memorized properties, from their earlier historical models. History does not begin with Rome, and, in many earlier cultures and episodes of human creative and self-creative work of earlier periods even before the rich Roman creative culture, this peculiarity of absolute authoritarian power of values created by human creative work also formed recognizable means of "dictate" of capital over individual characteristics and creative human beings. In all known earlier cultures, an active form of the influence of the narration of concentrated linguistic terms or written memory, a symbol for the contents of the value of human creative work, was constantly present and used. Throughout history, various languages, symbols, and written memories have become legal apologetic means that have been used as a process tool of human creative work and have been subordinate to the dominant capital accumulation and profit. Equally, they were and still are in the function of the social capital of the relationship that arose from the consumption of the presented use and traffic values of the increasingly abundant results of human creative current work. The dictate of the language, whether written or oral, was recognizable as an extremely pragmatic and clear authority to all. Most often in the form of linguistic forms, this is a unique tool and the human wage, everyday product recorded as rational to all acceptable maxims, formed in meaning or legal act, in "dicta", respected as an obligation of society as a whole to realize, preserve and constantly complement it. The oldest law and dicta that binds the entire social community originated before 2100-2050 BC before the birth of Christ and is known as the record of King UR-Namme in the Sumerian language. This law was written to assist the ruler in the permanent management of the Sumerian state. According to sources, this law was originally attributed in its origin to the gods, although other sources refer to Ur-Nammu's son Shulgin. The law mandated the conduct of all Sumerians, but also the punishments ranging from the death penalty to the mildest forms of fines to punish criminals. Laws, including the oldest one, which defines the behavior of the human community of the Sumerians, regularly in its basic characteristics as a means by which it was realized in pragmatic practice most often states and uses material value both as a reward and as a punishment taken away (or added) including loss of the greatest values in the possession of the human being, their life. Legal laws and systems as a dictate of the social life of communities include moral maxims of both legal and general moral features that have also been founded throughout history on the legal right to possession, accumulation of capital and profit. " Give the Emperor what belongs to him and give God what belongs to God" is irresistibly reminiscent of the modern trends in the social life of wage earners in the world, who are constantly taxed according to the written legal laws and the need to redirect the dominant capital.

Parallel to creative work as a feature and activity without which it is impossible in all earlier phases of its historical role, there is an absolute dictate of the value of total past work as a formed capital memorized by human labor as a categorical unconditional driver of creation and self-creation which in the beginnings of original human action manifests itself as an instinctive dictatorship with or without a conscious motive over one's own active, rational and willing being. Later, in organized communities, it has manifested as a dicta or rational dictate of capital in the possession of homo sapiens. The primordial instinctive animal-evolutionary dictate of active work and activity over time and with the help of an abundance of creative and self-creative activity and human work simultaneously changes human nature from instinctive to higher spheres of rational psych nervous action and the creation of rational activities dominated by the dictates of unconditional creation and self-creation of new values, both for themselves and for other participants in different social strata and contenders for capital, capital relations, and other values. The stratification of human labor into conditioned activities of higher forms of complexity arises with the emergence of primitive forms of capital accumulation that is capitalized within the sums of legal exploitation of other people's labor even in the earliest stages of primate social life. The principle of these primitive formations of accumulation and new capital with the right to some form of capital relations and organization of social reproduction which is known exclusively as the implementer of new organized conditioned current human work is identical in basic features throughout history and even today in the most complex forms of human creative and self-creative activity we know. Of course, its apparent legal characteristics at different stages of development are different in both quantitative and qualitative properties. Owners of legally acquired accumulation and capital only seemingly acquire their own independence from capital and accumulation dictatorship and necessary creative human activity which exclusively by new dictate creates new future successful accumulation and new capital based on other people's most dictated wage labor from which accumulation and capital emerge. The range of basic features of all strata of societies known to human history indicates the constant general subordination of entire communities created by the established rules of the dictatorship of capital, regardless of who its legal owner or creator is, whether an individual, group or society as a whole.

LEGAL SOURCE OF CAPITAL ACCUMULATION

The original fundamental features of the absolute dictate of capital arising from the current work of wage earners who conquered and directed human creative and self-creative work through the course of history as we know it is ensured by the legal exploitation of all values created by human labor and those that human labor consciously records from the richness of nature and with these recognizable value and use forms creates additional accumulation of capital for the benefit of its owner in the processes of earlier and modern history and probably in the near future are very similar and basically identical in their characteristics.

The most vivid and explicit evidence of these rules of existence of capital and its emergence from the course of live current work in modern legal acts on employment of world wage earners and their status wage characteristics is an exceptional source and guide for analytical records of the origin of accumulation and in general the origin of the newly created surplus value that forms the accumulation of capital and profit of capitalist, socialist other hybrid societies, just as in earlier history. Historically refined through a large number of variations in reproductive social systems and enriched by historical experience, modern social and legal features in the developed communities of the world that dominate the capital are completely identical throughout the creative history in one exceptional feature from which the whole known modernity and also the near future of mankind grows into its variations and values. We will cite the essential part of the legal definition in free interpretation that defines the relationship between the employer as the owner of capital and the entity that realizes the dictates of capital and the capital relation and the wage earner as a subject that we claim is the source of all created historical values generated by human creative work as we encounter it today in reproductive processes around the world. This essential part of the legal text, which by the nature of its rational description and dictate conditions and organizes us into a social labor force under the control of capital, is reduced in historical systems to the sentence: "whole work and values of creative work of a wage earner who is paid on the labor market, no matter how large or small, always belongs entirely to the employer or owner of capital who pays the wage earner and self-creator for his work on the labor market according to established criteria". Of course, this maxim is recognized in the political-economic formula of capital $C = VC / CC \times time$ or a given subject of work that is applicable to each phase of the historical development of mankind. To illustrate the essential part of this legal and immensely useful sentence, we will use a true event from the biography of two extremely important innovators in the field of electricity from the end of the 19th century and the beginning of the 20th century. N. Tesla, when he started working for Edison, was asked by Edison to complete and perfect the electric motor that Edison had formed, but he was not satisfied with his work. Edison promised that N. Tesla would pay $ 12 million if he succeeded. Tesla completed the project extremely successfully, but he never saw or received the money promised to him. What accrued to him after the project was completed was a $ 12 increase in his salary because he was an employee of Edison's company. In his explanation, Edison ironically told him that Tesla, as a man of European provenance, did not understand American humor. Edison's humor is an extremely clear and applicative legal farce of the existing historical reality and scene that explains the entire everyday life of current wage labor to its core. Shortly after that event, Tesla left Edison's company, devoting all his later work and creativity (700 patents) to the general welfare and prosperity of mankind and not to the accumulation of private capital, which was the basic but limiting thought of Edison's guide in his approach and understanding of inventive creative activity of Tesla, but also in general understanding of social relations formed by creative human work. Edison could not transcend the layer of dictatorship and capital culture that shaped him as a scientist and innovator, nor did he, from his dominant position of capital owner, have an understanding of the quantitative and qualitative value of labor and the contribution of each and even the most inventive worker simply because he completed every possible conversation about that newly created value and the new contribution of his employees or the growth of his "own accumulation" and "own capital" with a market wage, even though he was aware that it was the fruit of the work of his wage earners. Edison did not have a single legal reason to analyze the growth of his own accumulation and capital as Tesla's wage contribution, especially not as a contribution that exceeded Tesla's paid wage limits and required a completely different equivalent of his compensation and wages, since, in the then legal and moral (even today) codes, it did not exist. Other capital owners had never done this before Edison, nor do they do it today. On the other hand, in his cosmopolitan beliefs, Tesla, primarily as a scientist and innovator, as evidenced by the essential features of his inventions, overcame such a typical earthly orientation of innovation and science for the purpose of creating capital for private investment capital owners, pointing to a completely different symbiosis of science and humanity. In his statements, Tesla always pointed out that he used all his (accumulation, capital profit) savings and earnings only for the purpose of creating a better life for people and never for the purpose of creating his own wealth through the exploitation of other people's work. The scientist to whom probably all of humanity owed the most, especially the USA, died forgotten as a poor man in 1943 in New York. It is this city in which N. Tesla lived and worked throughout his megalopolis urban horizontal and vertical emergence during the late 19th and 20th centuries and even today that can thank Tesla's patents and the diversion of electricity from Edison's experimental impotent DC electric current frame to alternating unlimited electric force, which megalopolises and humanity really need. Tesla's patents and his creative work are still a source of enormous sums of capital accumulation and profit of private and corporate businesses who often do not know of Tesla's creative inventiveness nor that it is woven into their contemporary activities and creative work of all mankind.

In the initial moments of its early historical realization, this maxim we cited as the foundation of the modern production-reproduction capitalist and socialist world defined the geometric progression of the growth of accumulation and capital, but also the direction of modeling all social forms of values and relations between values by capital and the formation of new capital and capital relations. In particular, these historical processes based on the maxim we interpret have developed the roles of capital owners who have modeled the entire social process in which this past and current creative work of wage earners takes place in the same way as the maxim itself evolves into a universal principle, including modeling one's own and society's worldviews and visions of future creative and reproductive cycles as a constant of striving for an ever-increasing sum of the accumulation of capital and profit. In the same process, the (minimum and maximum) functional arithmetically set and dictated constant of wage labor is maintained, which guarantees (controlled by capital through wages) new creative ranges of use values and self-creation and reproductive function of the whole society (counties and the world) through geometric progression of accumulation of free capital in the possession of a smaller number of owners, which is mainly a consequence of "natural selection" within the total capital relation that allows the creation of legal social institutions and forms of government, again in the function of capital. The increasing concentration of capital has defined our urban, rural and industrial profiles of residence, but also the primary place of wage creative work, social life, disenfranchised market wage workers and capitalist wage earners, that is, private owners of large sums of capital on which the reproductive process of social communities still depends. It is especially important to note that this legal maxim with which we started this analysis and which employers and owners of dominant capital have at their disposal has created a

completely independent jurisdictional system from market
wage earners and their influence, which they have in the
process of creating and changing the legal system. Only
private owners of newly created accumulation, capital and
profit, or bureaucrats, as in known forms of socialism, cor-
respond to new chapters of the legal system as needed in
development strategies of capital and capital relations and
participate in those processes and procedures, in which
market wage earners often do not participate, since they do
not possess the right and authority of the dictates of capital
which is given and which models the whole social community. The right to dictate capital begins with higher sums
of capital with which it is possible to model the whole of
social reproduction. Such a modeled legal system, which
is primarily legal, not moral, and principled, has been elevated to the level of an omnipotent managerial tool with
which the almighty divine accumulation, capital and profit
from current wage labor are maintained. The owners of
this tool and dominant capital become at the same time
permanently conditioned uncritical poltroons of the dictates of omnipotent capital to which, unfortunately, in the
absence of other means for more efficient social reproductions in stereotypical behavior, the whole of humanity
aspires. Of course, the legal system serves all citizens and
all wage earners, provided that its use is interpreted by
apologists and its creators... lawyers of various specialties
of existing capital relations. The choice of a new and different legal interpretation, critique or change of the legal
order or its work in the parliaments of Western civilization
that breaks the layer and function of dominant capital in a

different worldview and understanding of reproductive socioeconomic functions in the current conditions is difficult to achieve from the doctrine of capital and capital relations encountered in megalopolis tic locations of powerful possessors of dominant capital around the world.

Still, "All roads lead to Rome." History has recorded and uttered this sentence as a landmark or, in modern jargon, marketing of general instructions for a successful life, to all citizens of the world. Primarily to emulate and learn how to be successful from Roman practice (an efficient megalopolis urban culture or a landmark for a successful capital relation) and pragmatic reality. Today, there are many megalopolises around the world, different in their historical genesis and cultural peculiarities, only similar to Rome of the same modern features created by wage labor and accumulation of capital in which huge overflows and concentrations of dominant capital created by the work of its wage producers are recognized domestically and around the world. The present time of our history belongs to the multiplied capital-defined hierarchy and urban megalopolis culture of the world. New York, London, Beijing, Shanghai Milan, Tokyo, Hong Kong, Moscow, Berlin, Paris, Singapore, Frankfurt, Chicago, and many other cities around the world are our goal of living and creative realization of all kinds.

Starting from the earliest and most primitive forms of wage labor for the owner of capital in the earliest history to the present day, the existential legal stability of this legal maxim has grown steadily until it became the foundation of even the most complex social systems of modern history. Regardless of the characteristics of political, legal, or economic systems throughout history in which we observe this maxim, it is regularly present as a fundamental and safe determinant of capital accumulation and economic reproductive processes. There is no known society and social order that does not use it. The use of human wage creative labor has more and more nuanced features, which is also the basis of their own creation and new and qualitative and quantitative achievements of an increasing number of wage earners around the world. It can be noticed that during the historical development of creative wage labor, the development of wage creative self-awareness is constantly growing, which increasingly wants direct management of the accumulation, capital and profit of its own work, which is currently managed and legally owned by privately owned and bureaucratic entities within the socio-economic systems that have appropriated this surplus value of wage labor through legal systems, with which they dictate the controlled framework of creative wage labor and its social being. Neither in earlier history nor today is a single wage earner hired to create new value, which is, unfortunately, from the perspective of the owner of dominant capital, his only meaning and historical role together with controlled consumption of wage value (other roles and functions are also subordinated to capital and capital relation but are significantly more out of focus function of capital), employed without the stated legal maxim being applied to his work and his social characteristics. This is the basic meaning of the historical contract between the capitalist and the wage earner, that is, the owner of capital and the wage earner who does not possess any free sums of capital and who offers his working and creative quality as capital through the market, with which he achieves socially dictated and respected participation by the owner of the capital for daily earnings. It is important to never forget that the contract with wage earners in the labor market, which is characterized by different rights and obligations of both wage earners and employers, is always market-defined in advance, and not only that, it is a direct consequence of previous accumulation of surplus value and capital of both past and current labor in the possession of the capitalist which provides him with a legal independent dictate of the use price of wage labor as any other useable commodity. The historical position of wage earners as it is today as well as the profile of the historical and humanistic being of mankind is a consequence of the legally appropriated value of his creative wage labor which was appropriated by geometric multiplications throughout history by the owner of dominant capital. In general, the exploitation of human labor as the exploitation of stronger capital with market instruments and other forms of modeling subordination to dominant capital is a fully cut scenario that grew out of the earlier history of the past work of wage earners. The principle of treatment of legal dominant capital towards all types of wage earners or less dominant capital is still completely identical to previous historical experiences and principled solutions. Today (information from 2017) according to the data of the World Bank, which are derived from the World Labor Organization, there are about 3,450,000,000 employed wage earners and about 250,000,000 unemployed wage earners in the world. All those who are employed acquire their status and social characteristics exclusively through the legal characteristic that we have tried to interpret with the help of the above maxim which characterizes and reveals the basic rights and position of wage earners in the production of newly created value. If the wage characteristics of our model and the maxim themselves were to place the owners of capital as wage earners (together with their private capital, no matter how large they were in the labor market or the investment market of the world), we would see a new additional layer of wages, in which owners of the capital, whether they want to or not, are recorded as obedient servants of the imperative pragmatic destiny of their own capital and its dictatorship in the same way as the largest population of poor wage earners in the world presented and quantified in the number 3,450,000,000 from the well-known World Labor Organization database. In the case of the owner of the capital, the maxim would have a slight modification that would certainly emphasize that each part of the recorded accumulated surplus value from the work of the broadest layers of wage earners and capitalist wage earners belongs to the newly created capital. In the maxim we encounter today, there is often an emphasis that the values of wage labor belong entirely to the employer and the owner of the initial capital. The fact that the newly created value belongs not only to the capitalist but also to his capital (social newly created value) means the past work of wage generations of earlier periods, which is even more evident in the case of the capitalist wage work. As before, in the initial content of the original maxim with which we tried to explain the relationship between wage earners and capitalist wage earners, so in recording the value of wage labor of the owner of dominant capital, the newly created value or new accumulation, formed capital and profit of all layers of wage earners are paid in a new amount of capital as a potential value that dictates any future wage creation in the new reproductive processes of modern societies. If this were not the case, no entrepreneurial work and creation would be considered productive creation and would be extensively meaningless. The management and recording of newly created value are also basically completed according to the logic of the right to possession, which is dictated by the amount of engaged capital that the economic entity has at its disposal. We will talk about that later. No wage earner, be it a poor disenfranchised market through a paid wage earner or the richest wage earner, the owner of capital who organizes and cares for the reproductive realization of his capital, is not a free creator today or during previous history. There are no free creators in the wage labor of the daily practice of accumulating capital and creating and supplementing capital relations, and there is no what is most similar to the freedom we most often imagine are the permanent processes of our creative and self-creative work that draw us to a particular understanding of freedom, but not its overall understanding or possession, since it is unavailable. The growth and understanding of freedom are enhanced by the memory of our past work and the current creative work of present generations. Of course, the dominant capital is unconditionally oriented to the possession of the total rational memory of humanity, especially that part of it which points to the creative and productive role of wage earners labor and its use that generates newly created value and accumulation. All uses of the total memory of mankind (information systems and databases) are under the control of capital, especially in the procedures of application of new conceptual creative interventions that require investment capital.

All wage earners are part of a vast vibrating organic body that develops, subordinated in the best possible way to the dictates of capital, whether these are owners or co-owners of large sums of dominant private capital or a smaller part of it, or exclusively owners of the use market capital of their own wage earning creative personality. Capitalist science and practice point us to just such an idea and socio-economic analytical cross-section of modern capitalist and socialist communities around the world. The wage capital of the lowest wage and capital characteristics is given to define its legal social characteristics as use capital through the labor market. Most wage earners achieve their reproduction by dictated working time, work task and market price as a reward for work, regardless of the value of their actual creative work under the control and dictates of dominant capital and which belongs to the owner or co-owners of engaged capital that cannot be reproduced without different profiles of wage labor purchased on the free market. No capital, small or large, can be realized in accumulation or new capital without human current creative and self-creation work. The newly created value that is the basis of future reproductive processes that arises on the basis of past work and live current work of wage earners is recorded as realized profit also through dictated criteria directed by dominant capital. The higher the dominant capital, the greater its influence on the complete local and world reproductive cycle. The primary task of dominant capital is to direct and control the reproductive and wage creative and self-creative cycle that ensures adequate accumulation and new capital, thus enabling every functional supplement and new cycle of functions of the favored capital relation without which it cannot survive. We often encounter in the jargon of everyday language around the world the term "world order". Everyone who uses the term knows that its scope and reach is given by the functions and pragmatics of accumulation and creation of new capital, primarily the most dominant capital of the world's economic superpowers, members of the trillion club led by the USA whose GDP exceeded 21 trillion dollars in 2019. The rest of the subordinated hierarchical pillar and the order of countries with lower GDP down to the lowest achieved results is subordinated to the world order of the dominant capital of the most developed countries in the world. Within the world order, there is a place of wage disenfranchised individual potential of both individuals without investment capital and those who make a profit through minimally available own investment in wage labor, thus achieving greater accumulation and capital than the usual market wage compensation typical for the world's largest population of wage earners. The range of qualitative and quantitative status characteristics of world wage earners is extremely large. All these data of the world order in the numerical representation of the relationship between GDP and per capita income or tax brackets can be followed in the very up-to-date statistics of world economic agencies or government analytical services around the world. What we have to judge ourselves and what we have to make our own rational and analytical judgments that are also part of our self-formation, because we are participants in these events, is everyday capital relation dictated by dominant capital through various forms of capital placement in subordinate wage earning communities around the world. Also, we must constantly analytically monitor the scope of capital relations and the typical properties and paths of capital that, in order to survive in this dictated relationship, of larger dominant capital conditionally used by less developed economic communities or countries of the world, promoting all capital relations of dominant capital, world order by their parliamentary "democratic" decisions. What we have to judge and what we have to make our own rational and analytical judgments about, which is also part of our self-formation, because we are participants in these events is everyday capital relation dictated by dominant capital through various forms of capital placement in subordinate wage communities. We also have to constantly analytically monitor the scope of capital relations and the typical properties and paths of capital that, in order to survive in this dictated relation of larger dominant capital, are conditionally used by less developed economic communities or countries of the world, promoting all capital relations of dominant capital, a world order by their parliamentary "democratic" decisions. From the perspective of wage earners who have exclusively the capital of their own market value living and working in an underdeveloped country with low GDP or low per capita income, the world order and the overall accomplishments of the most progressive achievements of humanity, both its immediate democratic environment and beyond, are much less accessible than are available to wage earners of the same peculiarities who live and work in the developed communities of the world, even though both are conditioned by a layer of the dictatorship of dominant capital. What they have in common is not only a per capita allowance but above all a fundamentally identical subordination to the reproductive functions of the dominant capital of the world without which they could not survive not only as a creative and self-creating being of new values conditioned by dominant capital, but very often as a living being.

This realized newly created dictated and controlled value in its emergence from the surplus value of wage labor belongs to the dominant capital which is also conditioned by the dictates and legal reproductive functions of accumulation, capital and profit which is superior to it and accompanies every step of reproductive cycles and often dictates unconditional violent behavior locally and significantly wider in the horrific aggressions of war destruction without any obligation to the millions of innocent victims, if the successful realization of a given or anticipated reproductive cycle in accordance with the world order is desired. Of course, it is proclaimed the legal progress of humanity with which at least in recent times the most developed countries of the world and their governments comply. The aggression of the dictatorship of capital has only one function and that is the unification and purification of retarded and unacceptable forms of creation of less developed communities of the world that are on the way to dominant capital. Probably deeper analyzes and assessments of our human behavior throughout history and today, which record human casualties and the causes of war, would indicate that capital and its acquisition is the basic motive for this mass and unpunished crime of human behavior that still continues legally and with impunity. There are far more innocent human victims as well as the devastating destruction of nature and cultural goods left behind by the "progressive ideologies" of the imperialist war in the name of capital in the 19th, 20th, 21st century, than any other natural or cosmic cataclysm known in human history. It is quite secondary whether you are defending or attacking in the name of capital (from capital) which is most often owned by a ridiculously small number of inhabitants (1% or less) on both sides of the conflict. It is important to note that the properties of dominant capital are often instructions for any criminal activity, and that most often all owners of capital, whether they are owners of dominant capital or holders of small amounts of capital, are responsible for these crimes. The dictate of the independent properties of capital, which defines us as an external force and the creativity of its owners, has

unlimited legal properties according to its size and dominance, which are enabled by the capital functions of legal
capital relations in the service of that capital, that the legal
systems in the parliaments of the countries of origin pro-
nounce completely legal in their performance and action.
The dictatorship of capital, which is, with its creative he-
reditary nature and predispositions, introduced into
socio-economic relations around the world, always has a
recognizable aggressiveness that dictates both universal
and particular and singular realization of all values into
accumulation through created surplus value from wage labor into new capital. The selfishly ruthless nature of the
capital that dictates every reproductive moment of the social communities of the world, groups and individuals is
the natural state and genesis of all history. "I", not "We",
is a person of capital who does not want to lose his own
property and clear and legal protection within the legal
system as well as all the realized values of private property. In addition, this "I" was formed by gradual
socialization processes by the same capital, regardless of
the large or small extent it created and accepted and to
whose dictates it voluntarily agreed, and that is its natural
social, cultural, political, legal and economic, primary and
secondary feature. The "I" is in fact an inconceivably large
concentrated rational capital in the endless process and
progress of geometric values. In the pyramid of dominant
capital, there is no place, at least not yet, for two different
ownership entities in the same place. There is a capital and
capital-exclusively defined private ownership dominance
that is constantly growing. "Everything flows" (panta

rhei), everything is a cosmic movement, as Heraclitus of Ephesus would say. This "I", in the general tangle of ego-centric characteristics and the environment of other individuals, both through the earlier history and values of past work and in modern capital relations of our civilizational communities and societies, is given to possess all the value primarily of the value created by "We", as usable productive market goods. "We" is composed of a multitude of reasonably disenfranchised capital of smaller values, thus directed to subordination and the market of dominant capital for the purpose of wage labor and the realization of its own survival. The wage being also belongs to the hierarchy of privately owned values, but to that part which is entirely controlled by the market reproductive criteria of dominant capital. However, we also mark wage market capital as a subject, as "I". "I" as a subject of wage disenfranchised live current labor or capital that appears on the labor market which is also the dominant owner of capital, the capitalist whom we marked as the superior subject of "I" due to the built dominant possession of values, and the whole civilization culture primarily and still marks as a means of use and a tool for its own purposes, and not as a producer of new social common values or as a subject of the historical emergence of all values. The wage earning creative and self-creative "I" of both singular and particular and universal characteristics is the subject of the entire origin of human history. The goal of every "I", both the large possessor of dominant capital and the small disenfranchised possessor of wage earners, is to create greater and greater accumulation by appropriating the surplus value from his own and others' work... to infinite universal greatness and values that are not limited by anything but creation and self-creation of other individuals ("I"), of course with identical intentions if he can realize them in his complete opposition to his advantage. If he does not make a profit, a chaotic state of subjective, particular and universal losses of the widest spectrum occurs, which another "I" appropriates as profit, because in the processes of growth of development and destruction of values, either material or ideological, in time and space of the universe nothing falls into irreversible nothingness. The "I" created by the previous creative and self-creative history at this stage of development today does not understand the common benefit of creative human work if it cannot possess it as a private owner in the form of capital. Other forms and meritorious features of people's social socializations throughout history are equally reluctantly accepted. The reason for this is the dominance of the primary features of the dictatorship of capital in which humanistic evolution recognizes it as a universal and particular and singular feature created by socialization as a dictated copy of all types and subtypes of the hierarchy of capital dictates and capital relations over human creative and self-creative work which surrounds and intentionally forms our capital "I" in everyday life. This is the essential reason for the failure of any revolutionary changes during human history that have been driven by rather sharpened qualitative democratic ideologies with the aim of returning the accumulation and capital created by human creative work at once and in a short time to its creators. Everything was in vain, without a quantitative and qualitative force that did not exist within the new post-revolutionary society. Adequate new and quantitative and qualitative strength needed by the new practice even with the majority and new goals of pro-revolutionary revolutionaries who were totally unprepared for the newly offered ideological foundations and practice of human creative work and creativity did not provide new rapid quantitative and qualitative growth of revolution-appropriate profiles. These circumstances and events are known companions in earlier and recent history and have regularly, at least until now, led to the failure of revolutions or the short duration of these historical episodes, which can be said to have relied more or less on the dictates of modest equity and most often on capital and capital ratio of the world environment in the form of investment loans, or some other lending and revitalization of social communities. And with the favor of the world economic system, which is often only the pragmatics of dominant capital in revolutionary transformations and experiments in history, the one who could not be a good master to use this well-known loan-sharking means of survival because there were no other means and tools of organization or only in the rudimentary beginnings, would regularly lose pace with the most developed countries of the world and their credit institutions. All communities of ambitious ideologies that bypass the dictates of capital and capital relations and capitalism and socialism have disappeared from historical processes, not because their ideological visions are unsuitable and scientifically inapplicable, but because of poor and inefficient economic practice and reproductive results achieved by these communities which cannot fight for a tolerant place in the world economic order within the relentless and perpetual competence of various more developed capitalist social communities and their aggressive dominant capital and capital relations, which are also equipped with countless strategies to control new, parallel capital relations that point to unwilling changes by dominant capital. Some emerging revolutionary communities, however, survived not only thanks to new ideologies and forms of organization and forms of recording the value of human creative work and a new way of using the accumulation of surplus value of the past work of their communities, but also the power of wage labor in the classical capital relation which enabled not only the creation of their capital and capital relation but also the world dominant capital which, through these communities, by various investments, realized primarily its own interests. Accepted by the whole community, legal social contract which "disposes" of daily pragmatic revolutionary and ideologically acceptable political force "authorized" by the Constitution and other fundamental laws by the whole community in the people's parliament to manage capital and capital relations of the whole society, is the foundation of the legal process and practice of creation that we know today in the form of the dominant "I". As much as it tried not to do so in modern capitalism and socialism in organized everyday recognizable practice, "I" is the subject of history, "I" is the dominant capital and capital relation, which is the real organized protagonist of events throughout history. It is also a permanent dictator and controller of the versatile creative and self-creative work of individuals in the daily wage functions found imposed by its socialized sharpened hierarchy of capital dictates and capital relations of which it is a private owner. Regardless of the fact that individualism is stimulated in the public legal heritage of the entire history and especially in the modern ideology of liberal capitalism which is the foundation of modernity in general, it is increasingly noticed that the organized dictatorship of capital within the legal political and economic system (rule of law) which capitalism and socialism possess as the basic means of survival (although it is essentially available in practice to a very small number of owners 0.1%), that the free development of individualism for all, especially the form that goes hand in hand with dominant capital is actually limited and controlled by the same dominant self "I" which is formed and socialized not only as a solitary subject but also as part of the wage subjects and functions of the broadest masses in the reproductive cycles in modern social relations which we call the capital relation. "I" as the private or bureaucratically political possessor of dominant capital is the legal possessor of the whole rhythm of the socio-economic dictate of capital which that same capital whose owner is also a given dictate in an abstract given size is constantly obsessed with until its planned realization. Each reproductive cycle is reduced to a dictated, though not fully mastered, vices circle "circulus vicious" that grows more or less in its quantitative and qualitative scope for both the wage-earning owner and the market wage earner of modern liberal capitalism.

How the development and presence of the "I" of wage earners as the equivalent of dictated capital in practice as creative individualism is visible in both quantitative and qualitative terms can be judged only by analytical figures from tax bracket statistics and GDP cross-sections of countries to which wage earners belong.

The scale of the widest spectrum of socialized wage individualism and its features that enable it in the modern world has a huge range and countless attributes that originate from the deepest historical genesis and from modern and self-acquired conditions of self-realization into a creative and self-creative being. My goal is not to deal with statistics from the world balance sheets of different countries that reflect the position and overall scale of wages of their countries, but one of the key attributes for understanding the effectiveness of individualism of wage earners to be accepted as an active "I" is its wealth and capital that forces it to dictate and which enables it in the social relation between other individual subjects both closer to the primary group and in the secondary or any particular forms of social organization to which it belongs during its creative and self-creative work and life. Statistics of property and wealth possessed by world wage earners generally indicate that the vast majority of world wage earners are poor and without significant possessions of any kind, and the individualism available to them is directed primarily at mere wages to ensure the survival of their own working and self-created beings or members of narrow primary group to which they belong. The entrepreneurial achievements of most wage earners presented in world statistics are very modest and their individualism and creative work ability are most often tied to the more dominant capital to which they belong as wage earners in daily current work. The general inequality and stratification of the social communities of the modern capitalist world into the extremely rich and extremely poor not only worries the poor strata of wage populations but also the richest strata (which we also define as wage earners) of the owners of dominant capital. However, it is necessary to emphasize that, regardless of the unstoppable and aggressive nature of the growth of dominant capital, the second most common accompaniment to the stratification of social communities into a small number of rich "I" and a large number of poor "I", is in fact greed and a complete lack of general moral and ethical and principled elements and criteria which would be constantly created and harmonized with the universal and with the social and individual characteristics of the values created on the basis of creative and self-creative current work. The constant source of general pragmatic moral maxims essentially does not exist as a creative automatism of the social processes of the current work of the creator's wage earners. Ethical maxims of universal significance are suppressed by strong legality protected by dominant capital, which is particular or singular in character. Universal ethical norms and their emergence are still present in our creative current work and are an integral part of creative and self-creative processes of human past work and its current work in which they appear not only subjectively but as a universal principle of reality that does not transcend and await us somewhere far away on the horizon. In our cultures and social relations built by the dictates of capital, the right of the stronger (the right of dominant capital) and its modern apologetic marketing policy, scenography, lie and illusion in which millions of generations are born and live, created and die with a modest profile of individualism still dominate.

SUCCESSFUL REVOLUTIONS

Symbiotic and adaptable modern China is an ideal example of a relatively successful revolutionary environment in the processes of change over the last 30 years. This one-party control of capital and the control of newly created value in China in general does not abolish the profile of capital and capital relations but plans and realizes it in different controlled and planned reproductive conditions. Without a qualitatively and quantitatively new capital relation, and without the right to creatively manage surpluses from surplus value, that is, the management of capital accumulation and profit, Chinese wage earners are like the wage earners of modern capitalism. Likewise, the other social and productive characteristics and status we recognize in its 800,000,000 million wage earning population do not in fact indicate almost any quantitative or qualitative aspiration for completely new socialist reforms of China's non-ownership attitude towards capital, the accumulation of profit they generate. What is noticeable in modern China at first glance is primarily a centralized form of capital control and capital relations within social reproductions based on cheap wage earners capital that is always available to the one-party socialist system just like the wage earners of capitalist countries in the labor market are regularly available to dominant capital. China's wage population is not just Chinese variable capital available to the Chinese Communist Party. Like any world variable capital, Chinese wage earners are also a significant part of world variable wage capital bought out but also moved away in part or in full participation in the management of newly created value by world investors in Chinese manufacturing everyday life. Chinese wage earners capital (variable capital, human creative and self-creative work) is subordinated to countless corporate affairs around the world that are present in China precisely because of the reasonable dictates of the world's dominant capital (accumulation of own earnings) which China's official political reality accepts as symbiotic capital which is realized in the accumulation and profit through the conditioned cheap wage of the Chinese wage earner who is thus a permanent source of surplus value and the accumulation of Chinese and world dominant capital present in the reproduction cycles of China and the world corporations present in China today.

China's extremely large, cheap, and usable wage-earning population is its own and the world's source of capital accumulation. According to GDP statistics and data around the world, China is the world's second largest economic power not only because of the capital it has formed from the creative work of its domestic wage earners within

China but also because of the huge investment of its free capital from Chinese wage labor in the economy of Asia, Africa, South and North America, Europe and other countries of the world that gladly receive the capital of other communities of the world in accordance with the rules of the world economy. There are a large number of such social communities with more modest economic balances and reproductive characteristics that gladly receive investment aid not only from China but also from other investors in the world, including Eastern European countries, which previously belonged to capital and capital relations of bureaucratic socialism on the model and under the control of the USSR. Today, these countries are emerging capitalist communities like the "runaway penitent son and a returnee to history" Russia, Poland, the Czech Republic, Slovakia, Hungary, Romania, Moldova, East Germany, Slovenia, Croatia, Bosnia and Herzegovina, Montenegro, Serbia, Macedonia, Albania, Bulgaria and many other countries. What should be added to this group of countries of the former socialist states are certainly capitalist countries around the world that have similar or identical characteristics and difficulties in their development. The transition from one capital relation to another capital relation or the transition from a known to another reproductive production feature that is not experienced within the hierarchy of the world's dominant capital, of course, does not guarantee the successful development of these new communities. Ambitious ideological illusions and uncritical imitations and plagiarism of developed capitalism are often not realized, as the practice of new countries created after 1990 not only in

Europe but also elsewhere, points out in the GDP balances of these countries for the last thirty years since the fall of the Berlin Wall. It is this group of countries together with China in its latest commitments that proves that human civilization has not yet developed its creative work and does not have a better means and tools than the traditional formation of accumulation from current wage labor and the assistance of the legal maxim which conditions the market wage earner to work for dominant capital and to use all the advantages of capital and the capital relations of the capitalist economy and the capitalist reproductive relations. On the other hand, it can also be concluded that the early world socialism of the 20th and 21st centuries in all its forms lost, at least for now, the battle to prove itself as a powerful means of democratic change but also for new solutions and forms of accumulation and creation of capital as social property or non-property social relations as it announced in its revolutionary appearances and ideological doctrine. We must also not forget that the natural abode of socialism and all its old and new features is woven into the modern capitalist currents of democratic parties and programs throughout world parliaments as the foundation of lasting democratic processes and commitments awaiting a suitable historical moment for their realization. When it comes to this fateful companion and the daily presence of socialism, the world's dominant capital takes care of it by acting on this movement with rigorous control within the entire world political, legal, and economic process in its favor....

It can also be concluded that the world is threatened by almost no immediate danger from socialism or communism because there are no more serious democratic forces that would realize such ideologies and social systems in modern practice of more successful creative and self-creative practices better and more pragmatically than the existing capital-dictated social relations to the general satisfaction of all market wage earners of the world as well as capitalist wage earners. Different legal approaches and commitments of world wage earners in relation to the vision of their future development and the way to use production rights and duties and dispose of surplus value, accumulation, capital and profit, in the future will be mostly located in capitalist communities where they originally belong and where they were conceived long ago in the sources of capitalist revolutions around the world. We hope that modern capitalism will realize in the foreseeable future that the position of wage earners or the revitalization and growth of quantitative and qualitative value and the role of variable capital is an essential part not only of dictated capital but also of anticipated far greater newly created value which is essential and that, in order to achieve this goal, they must necessarily create much better conditions for socialization and standards of acquiring creative knowledge and a better life for the majority of the wage population, especially the extremely creative wage earners of the world. By investing in the quantitative and qualitative values of variable capital, the accelerated development of all socio-economic functions of wage earners, even in the dictatorship of capital, capital will grow much faster and be more accessible to its owners and society as a whole. Some call its socialism and even communism, but in our daily processes under the control and dictate of capital we are still extremely far from that theoretical model of socialist-communist welfare that no one is familiar with in practice. All socialist revolutions are essentially at least until now only forms of capitalist reforms and changes that did not last long unless they developed a specific and dominant capital relation for their own survival and competitive place within the world order. Socialist reforms and revolutionary influences in the last two centuries are far more present within modern capitalism rather than as independent social communities. It seems that they will remain there, supplementing their progress with the progress of the creative and self-creative work of the capitalist wage earners.

VISIONS OF CAPITALISTIC REFORMS

The essential origins of capital accumulation from past and contemporary current work of world wage earners described in our maxim in an earlier text that we can find in world banks and world national and international corporations that dictate capital functions are not discussed often and not in the way they are presented in this exposition. Likewise, modern econometrics does not use the features with which one can see the influence and significance of human creative work of wage earners for the emergence of new accumulation and new capital. What is important for our attention in this part of the text is the statement that; a) the wage earner regularly produces use value intended for the market and consumption, b) he produces more use values if he works harder, c) the use value of wage capital through creative work and practice is constantly growing which is recognized by the owner of capital and capital relations only if wage earners create MORE than they are paid on the labor market, otherwise their use value disappears or is replaced by the demanding side of capital by a more efficient wage force (cheaper, more capable of producing new use values), a technique or technological process that completely or partially replaces the human wage function d) there is a big difference for the dominant and independent capital of the world that models us between the production of use values intended for the market within a corporation as part of the reproductive system and the production of use values in the general reproductive relationship of the whole society or attempts to control both the production and consumption of larger social communities and the whole world. The beginnings of the world's expanded reproductive control have long been in the form of absolutely dominant capital of the most developed countries in the world, which through investment borrowing of smaller economic powers and communities control their growth and development and the impact on capital dominance of the richest countries of the world. Although dominant capital does not come from one country or center but from different countries or institutions that have global significance on its behalf, the principled function of capital is definitely in line with the top achievements of modern doctrines of capital relations protected in international law and codes. Disagreements of uncoordinated action of capital are commonplace but no one in the hierarchy of dominant capital which defines borrowers and debtors gives up on acquired new capital and accumulation values won into capital relation that is passionately believed in and possible. This permanent 'perpetual motion' of the geometric progression of capital is maintained by the wage-earning population of the world by essentially creative human labor under the control of world capital and capital relations. It is the duty of the world's wage earners in this growing vortex to create a new use value that is easy to cash in and form into new capital. The dominant world capital that dictates this creative and self-creative work and the duty paid by wages, plans and anticipates that this wage labor, in addition to the newly created use value of wage labor, will also create accumulation and new free capital with which to enter a new reproductive cycle. These cycles will be realized regularly and in the indefinite future, as there is no other choice for now. No penny of indebted or invested capital within the existing capital of world relations is returned within the debt relations of modern economies unless a new newly created use value is created through wage earners past and current labor. Of course, through various mortgages, creditors ensure that debt collection can also be made from other sources of previously materialized past labor or natural resources of debtors. A general illustration of the annual or multiannual reproduction cycles of world capital as well as of corporate business indicates the state in which each subsequent socioeconomic reproduction is successful if it covers with the remainder (accumulation of capital) the previous reproduction cycle.

The production of use values controlled by corporate capital within expanded reproduction within any state, federation or world is also consumption and aims to direct and anticipate complete control of all conditions of production of new values, especially wage creative and self-creative work, which is the source of all emerging use values of social communities in which the total and wage earning population and its consumption become a balanced cause of the simultaneous harmony of production and consumption. The surplus value of wage labor is constantly monitored and controlled, which must always create a higher value than the price of the market wage value at which it is paid and which is given to it as the minimum value by the dictates of capital. In addition, wage earners must constantly prove that the growth of their usable creative value and usability is conditioned by the dictates of capital, so that always ambitious capital and capital relations can generally arise on a larger scale and be in the function of capital accumulation and also in the general social function. This new amount, which records the surplus value from wage labor, always forms a new, more ambitious capital and again enables a new expanded social reproduction and a new broader and more thorough control of the social communities of the world. Cycles of social reproductions are recognized as extended, which is the optimal variant, but also as simple and reduced cycles of socio-economic development. This very often depends on the interaction and aggressiveness of capital and capital relations in which similar production programs have both weaker and stronger reproductive communities that are realized on the local and world markets.

One of the questions that arises from the analytical approach to the previously stated legal maxim that defines the current position of use (capital) value of wage earners and the position of employer wage earners or owners of capital in relation to the use value of wage earners and all other use values necessary to produce new use values: did the complete newly created capital and accumulation really originate only in wage creative work or is there some other creative source of new capital and accumulation? Commenting on this question, although in the scientific context it seems simple, does not oblige anyone from the modern pragmatic, productive public, especially the most powerful and developed countries in the world, to give a definite answer. To repeat the modern capitalist economy without which the world obviously cannot do, which grows out of the nature of the dictates of capital and capital relations owned by a small number of capitalist wage earners who control and use it for their own purposes, uses only the use-value of human creative work which creates more value than invested, not only in wage capital but in the overall process of production and social reproduction. As unbelievable as it may seem, the main reason that there are no better means for the progress and creative growth of humanity than the dictates of capital, capital relations and wage labor lies in the fact that better means in the existing creative and self-creative historical moment and process are not known nor is there any back-up variant even as a necessary evil that could be of use. All human creative forces and in all creative fields are woven into the flows of dominant capital and capital relations.

However, it is noticed on a daily basis that the optimism of current and future creative achievements of science, education, technology and technical achievements created by the past and current work of wage earners has an increasing share in the scope and reach of creative and independent processes of modern current work which significantly affects new roles and the importance of capital in reproductive cycles. It is obvious that capital as well as capital relations cannot survive without creative ongoing human labor, which is increasingly becoming a decisive factor in the entire reproductive cycle and pushing traditional independent capital dictates and ideological explanations into the background. Accumulated capital from past current work of earlier periods creates the conditions for the realization of the necessary profile of creative work without which it cannot survive and is increasingly close in this symbiosis with creative human work like inseparable Siamese twins who cannot survive otherwise. In other respects, each of us has accumulated the value of past work, but also the value of our own current live work.

Primarily, I have in mind the most radical roles of creative work, which for their rational and universal survival need newly created value but do not need a capital relation and accumulation of private capital that belongs to a few but to all its creators who participate in its creation. Evidence of the growth and ever-increasing influence of world wage earners on reproductive cycles is reflected in the ever-increasing participation of wage earners in the political life of social communities, which is growing even in the most conservative political systems that make it impossible in various ways. It is also a signpost of wage political and historical commitment to return accumulation and capital to its creators in the future. This long-lasting process that will form a new use value of wage creative capital is still at its early stage. Today and in the foreseeable future, decisions on reproductive cycles and creative work of wage earners will most often be made within a small group of legal private owners of capital, or their managers, which in a way indicates a totally irrational and absurd state of consciousness by which minority controls the humanity, but different application of capital, especially dominant capital and its legal, political and economic system which maintains it does not exist or is present in limited sporadic affairs. Incomplete potential of creative and self-creative work of wage earners necessary for capital, illustrated by the current state of controlled and unused predispositions of the wage majority limited by capital, which is constantly present in the creative and self-creative past and current work of the wage earner will certainly change whether the legal owners of the capital want it or not. The stolen history of human creative and self-creative work, as well as the associated accumulation of newly created capital, must return to its original place, human creative work. The only means to ensure this goal is a new quality and quantum of wage creative work.

However, let us go back to our maxim that originally marks every wage earner in the world. Within this maxim that we have stated and used by all legal systems of the world and which defines the status and job characteristics of wage earners in the modern world (but also earlier in the history of overall past work) it is noticeable that we have three basic relatively independent entities. These are capital (past labor), capital owner and wage earner (current labor). Two subjects are living human creative and self-creating beings, capitalists and wage earners and we can place them in the category of everyday wage earners, while the third, which we call capital which is an active material and metaphysical subject and as such anticipates in itself and its sum feasibility the creative work of its own augmentation secured by the geometric progression of the new wage creation. It is the motive, dictate and anticipation of new values that everyone strives for in all models of human creation in the entire historical reality. Its appearance and existential presence through human creative work and the language of active creators and self-creators is constantly transformed into a culture of dominant social values which is respected by all members of society through interaction.

Capital is not only an economic value that we denote by generally accepted infinite variations of monetary values, it is also a representative of various sets of singular, particular, and universal values derived from human labor, capital is itself a creative human personality. As world capital, it represents the sum of the achievements of human wage labor in the social relations of production and consumption created during the historical processes of creation and self-creation of all mankind. These sums are most often presented in a relatively fluid exponential monetary sum. Beyond this usual representation of operating capital and the total values of human creative and self-creative work, there are endless areas of as yet unrecorded creative values in the alternatives of capital in the process and actions of creators that will be recorded at another time. Capital in the universal sense is constantly read as the infinite potential of the sum of past human creative work. The growth of total human wealth throughout history depends on the harmony of human creative and self-creative work and the sum of not only the free pragmatic operating capital of its owners but also the total set of social values created by past current work of previous generations recorded in the general wealth of comprehensive human culture. Capital tends, in addition to being singular or particular, to be as universal as its creators, the wage earners. On this path of identification with the universal properties of the infinite universe to modern imperfect humanity that does not reach the universal, there are two essential obstacles a) understanding the movement of the universe and b) it is necessary to build a new valuation of creative human labor other than market wage capital relations. With its future achievements from the arsenal of its creative and self-creation, the human species will increasingly allocate and use those means and fundamental values that will enable its being a gradual compatible transition into a universal and rational human creative being without capital and capital relations. This is not and cannot be the task of just one generation of creators and wage earners as is commonly thought. Nevertheless, each generation contributes and records its contribution to this process, which is especially visible in recent history and the extraordinary growth of the quantity of wage earners, but also their creative and self-creative qualities.

All three subjects and the wage earner and the capitalist and capital are an inseparable part of the creative processes of creation and self-creation. The independent existence of any entity from this trinity is impossible at any time or in the socio-political system known to history. Just as neither Egyptian, Greek nor Roman culture and state, no matter how rich, would ever create any new value or new wealth of their own cultures based on past work, without conditioned and dictated current wage (slave) work, nor would they achieve the accumulation of sufficient operating capital for future development, so modern capitalist and socialist states, regardless of wealth and total historical heritage, would also not achieve any accumulation of capital or form the operating capital of future reproductions without conditioned and dictated work of wage earners who are not only the initiator of active functions of this trinity of capital, its owner and the wage earners themselves, but also its direct creator. To better understand this, imagine the situation and the result that we usually record in monetary value for the annual work of wage earners and owners or managers with capital shown in GDP (gross domestic product) for each country for example for the

United States, England, Germany, China, Japan, France or any other economic power or superpower of the world. Without conditional wage earners within the USA but also wage earners around the world employed in American free capital projects (or capital of any other nation in the world) and their work... GDP of USA would be equal to "0". And it does not represent an unknown in the progression of the creation of future values of labor and its role which primarily forms the accumulation of new values and new capital for its owners or managers of future reproductive developments. On the other hand, we can follow the inseparability of these three entities by imagining the situation among the wage earners of the most developed countries in the world if someone removed from their environment all capital and its legal owners and managers and all capital functions that previously existed and formed productive communities. The GDP of such communities would also be a catastrophic "0". Tragic experiences from the microeconomic spheres for such a presentation of the link between capital and wage labor abound in migratory investment transactions and the modern fluid movement of financial capital around the world that does not need a passport or visa for its cosmopolitan travels illustrates the suffering of communities due to capital to all policies and ideologies. It is equally clear that the third part of the unity of the subjects we write about, which we have marked as capital, both operational and capital as the overall culture of creating social communities in our notions and ideas, could not survive on its own without its owners - wage earning capitalists and the wage earning creators who are not its owners or managers and who ensure its accumulation and formation, thus showing further increase and pragmatic progress. The peculiarity of social culture as a dictated creative and self-creative dominant social profile and capital relation, is that such communities that cannot reproduce and renew capital and capital relation would disappear entirely from historical currents, which can be further illustrated by dramatic historical and contemporary events and the disappearance of great Assyrian cultures and traditions , Egypt, India, Ancient China, Greece, Rome, Maya, Incas, Aztecs, or contemporary and many other cultures of the world and communities in contemporary creative and self-creative processes of monopoly imperialist or Nazi capitalism or bureaucratic socialism of recent date. If only the owners of capital disappeared from this trinity and the well-known creative culture with revolutionary changes, the complete legal, political, and economic system as we know it would disappear. We know this kind of revolutionary change in the practice of socialism, but only as a transformation of private property relations into bureaucratic forms of manipulation of capital relation that did not bring good results to social and civilizational development for the simple reason that private property of earlier systems of capitalism social ownership without the creation of capital and capital relations has changed significantly, nor have these changes grown into a superior creative work process that has promoted socialist communities into the most developed economic powers in the world. On the other hand, we must not forget that even if socialism developed as a complete world process or revolution, it could not survive without using the dictates of capital and capital relations (bureaucratic control) within its developmental reproductive planning goals. Historical currents and experiences lead us to the conclusion that we are constantly convinced that our visions of the historical models of just societies we want must be, in addition to being in scientific models, built in pragmatic practice in order to be real and common. In other words, they must possess the dominant pragmatic practice of the overall creative work processes of all creators and self-creators. Such a thorough and independent possession of past and live current work requires far more complex social relations for which humanity is not ready today because the hitherto built foundations of quality and quantity of human creative work as a historical heritage independent of capital and capital relations have not been created.

ESSENTIAL CAUSE OF THE SYMBIOSIS OF CAPITAL, WAGE EARNING CAPITALIST AND MARKET WAGE EARNER

The answer that could clarify the questionable title is essentially simple in general terms and could be applied to any owner who owns investment capital and an unconditional obligation to fertilize it in one of countless ways in an existing capital relation. The essential cause of the symbiosis of capital and wage earners begins in the general motion of the matter of the universe and manifests itself as an evolutionarily compatible property of the matter of the human being in its early stages of development by an irresistible active instinct to achieve various goals. And in the later stage of development, as a feature of symbiosis awareness and memory of past creative work and the values of creative human work, a rational planning vision was realized through dictated and organized human creative and self-creative work, thus becoming the most effective means by which the human species consciously created new use value primarily of itself and satisfied its needs of the most varied kinds. In a way, instinct and categorically fatal creation generated a culture of capital dictates by transitioning from nervous to psych nervous activity. Unfortunately, the historical trends in the development of human creative and self-creative work are not absolutely free, nor are we familiar with the social systems of free creators, but are exclusively organized by dictated values according to the principle that and the conditionality towards a new total creative and self-creative capital as a culture not only for the general survival of the Planet Earth and the universe, but for a permanent creative sojourn in the culture of work as its essential feature on the Planet Earth and in the universe. The creative work of the human creative and self-creative being is always superior to the static complexity of the dictates of the capital that uses it, especially if the capital is owned by a small number of owners. It is this possessive static dictatorship of capital that is processed by legal systems that are constantly refined according to need, an indication of its weaknesses and incompatible relationship with the movement of the universe that indicates its abolition in its current state.

Expansion of creative human work and self-creation to be as efficient and free as it can be, cannot be limited by any means, especially not by the means created by a powerful extremely small section of the human population to control and subjugate most wage creative ongoing work and creation to their own interests and exclusively to its narrower creative vision imposed in both production and consumption within the cycle social reproductions as the only practice and reality. Unfortunately, the whole humanity and all its smaller particular communities or states of the modern world are precisely in this historical phase of the dominant dictate of dominant capital. Modernity is today marked by capital as a tool with which human creative work is dictated, but also with the characteristics and growth of parallel intolerance shown for the existing state and functions of capital and its social institutions by human creative wage labor, especially in relation to capital accumulation, profit and its management.

The larger the capital, the more it depends on wage labor in its performance and direction of social life and general creativity. Capital as an independent subject is a potential but it does not have its own independence and independent freedom. Its existence is not possible without wage earners labor. The total potential freedom of capital and the total freedom of the creative work of mankind have an imperative tendency to fully identify themselves into a single subject compatible and appropriate to the universal movement in the future.

Modern private capital has the same characteristics in all its developmental fluidity, which in this phase of the development of human creative work still does not show universal and general tendencies, but particular features that we recognize as a private ownership relation. The larger the capital or the more it is in private possession, the freer it is, at the same time it is more and more dependent on the development of wage creative and self-creative work. However, it should be emphasized that the meaning of private ownership in this context is not exclusively related to the possession of dominant capital but to the possession of each part of it within the reproductive hierarchy and its functions. In particular, we want to stress the importance of the possession of capital in the possession of the wage subject which is the source of creative work and thus the overall freedom of social communities. In existing societies that we know the smaller the capital, the less free it is, and the more often it escapes freedom as an opportunity to dictate a more significant capital relation (legal, political, and economic system as capital) or even its own wage labor. The constant increase in the demanding needs of human creative and self-creative work tends to integrate into the creative process itself all the values and all the past and all the current work of each reproductive cycle. Likewise, the minimal functions of private and socially owned institutions in the contribution and flow of complex processes of creation and self-creation of modern wage earners, to whom the future has assigned a different name, which will eventually be achieved, can already be seen today. Over time, wage earners will become permanent rational creative creators without the controlled bureaucratic functions of the legal economic and political system, regardless of who creates and owns them as a means of capital relations.

The modern reality of the life of individuals and social communities in general, which is marked by the creative and self-creative work of human communities, does not exist without a rational planned existing and anticipated dictatorship and vision of existing capital, which directs and creates new capital which may or may not be known to all participants in the process in its principled features that appear in countless forms of creativity and political forms of social life both today and earlier history. The creation of new social communities without the dictatorship of capital is not possible in the current trends of development of the social communities of humanity that are known to us. Equally, the creation of a completely new history without capital and capital relations in the social communities of the world "ab Ovo" (from the beginning) is impossible. The main reason for this is the lack of an appropriate level of creative culture and a significantly higher level of wealth of means of production that would allow it. In other words, humanity has not yet created either particular or universal means of eliminating capital and capital relations and achieved new, more efficient, and fruitful means for its creative present and future. We see this best in recent history in the short historical duration of inefficient dictatorships of the proletariat, various socialist forms of government or autarchic national and nationalist (often Nazi and fascist) forms of capitalist economy that represent these utopian intentions and aspirations. We can follow the same processes within the most developed forms of capitalism in the processes of stratification of monopoly and imperial and colonial economies, which are in principle condemned as an evil of capitalist business and economy by both capitalist and socialist visionaries. Essentially monopolistic economy as well as imperialism, rejecting its primary evolutionary features arising from the dictates of capital in the earlier stages of capitalism, embraced other and much more sophisticated means typical of modern flows of capital relations that guarantee the accumulation of capital created by human wage labor. During the 20th and 21st centuries, new radical forms of association and symbiosis of dominant capital emerged and of course new forms of dominant monopolies and imperialism, especially in the financial capital sector owned by members of the trillion club of the world's richest countries. On the other hand, a large part of radical systems do not survive on the historical stage in their particular micro-cosmic environments due to their static conditioned and closed nature of creating their own capital ("ab Ovo") without cooperation with the environment. In these circumstances of creating new more fertile capital relations different from the traditional forms of accumulation and in parallel with the existing traditional systems of dominant capital, which is regularly much more efficient in its functions, the new radical society was doomed in advance. Due to the inefficient creation of new different means and social relations of production and general creativity with which they would be noticeable and respected in their efforts to climb the ladder of world dominance, capitalist, socialist or hybrid communities are disappearing from the world stage, which indicates the importance of the primary pragmatic features of nurtured pragmatic capital relations that are in this eternal process a relentless competitor, especially towards the new unknown and experientially incomplete revolutionary communities. Superficial understanding of K. Marx's scientific analysis and Marxism, by authors and apologists of socialist development as well as other scientific theories, policies, economics, sociological analyzes and other sciences used in the formation of new and ambitious socialist-capitalist communities as a basis and alibi for general commitment towards better social communities and a fruitful future in many state communities of the modern world in recent history has left in practice the disastrous and long-lasting consequences not only for new development but also for the basic and usual pragmatic rehabilitation of decent reproduction of these communities. Of course, the rights to experimental and creative new form of communities and modern new interventions in social relations of production and improvement of the existing state are eternal and welcome part of creative anticipations towards new and more efficient creative endeavors of human communities regardless of age within modern pragmatic practice around the world. However, these experiments are often an expensive and illusory departure from the unattainable ideals offered by uncritical political marketing, which are ultimately chosen by the wage earners of these communities according to their level of awareness and understanding of the dictatorship of the dominant capital to which they want or do not belong. This is especially true when it comes to those revolutionary experiments which, in their nature of survival and commitment, are entirely contrary to the dictates and arbitration of the dominant world capital present throughout the world and in various ways dominates the world economy and general social development.

The suffering and stagnation of these communities is regularly long-lasting and extremely large-scale. The intention of this part of the text is not to point to the very scarce revolutionary future of any radical idea of the future, but primarily to the relentless dictates of world dominant capital that controls every new form of creative human work, including the theory and practice of contemporary sociopolitical change. The most severe consequences of domination and control of dominant capital around the world are recognizable in the public life and work functions of wage earners around the world who are constantly dosed with pragmatics in favor of capital through legal systems that ensure maximum accumulation of capital to its owners, which are the richest countries of the world (the so-called trillion club of countries whose GDP exceeds trillion values). At the same time, modern capitalist pragmatism often does not take even the slightest care about the humane living conditions and self-creation of the capital and individual function of individual wage earners, their families, all types of primary groups and entire social communities of the world's wage earners and societies as a whole. A more harmonious balance than the existing humanistic socialization and capital relations we know will only harmonize the future through creative human labor that will eliminate the creation of accumulation and private property through the dictates of dominant capital over wage creative work and reproductive processes of social communities. Human history has created a creative homo sapiens through gradual processes of self-creation using constantly creative work and new more modern means of work, and this detail is extremely important and provides an opportunity to point out how this phenomenon a revolution of human creative work which can be abolished in its development only by a destructive cataclysm unknown to us. Contemporary human history, although under the dictates of capital and apologetic legal systems of capital relations, is still an independent creative wage revolution that flows, made possible by the act of free creative human labor.

FINANCIAL CAPITAL

During the historical development of capitalism, but also much earlier, many traces of various forms of entrepreneurial activity and capital formation could be seen, which are recognized in the properties of a comprehensive centralized dictatorship of capital within reproductive systems that initiates partial or most frequent massively growing reproductive cycles whose goal is to create new larger accumulations of capital than spent in favor of the initial dominant capital. Capitalism and other social systems we know have managed to preserve the function of capital and capital relations thanks to its very nature, which most often during its development and enlargement is promoted and nurtured into a sharpened unconditional centralized instrument of dictates of all historical and contemporary values which have become an integral part of the socialization of every human being. This dictate and conditionality from its own being is constantly transferred by capital to its creator, to the wage-earning population of human creative work, dictating and forming the overall socialization. None of the manifestations of the dictatorship of capital in the reproductive processes of the world is as illustrative but also current in everyday life as the power of the dictates of financial capital of the dominant capitalist superpowers of the trillion clubs of the most developed countries. Financial capital today represents an essentially freely formed loan-sharking profit generated and accumulated in the capital relation from the past materialized and current work of wage earners. Under special circumstances, this capital is given for use to the existing reproduction systems of enterprises, international corporations, banking system, states and other business entities that need it. The function of financial capital is dictated by legal systems built during earlier history. Like most legal laws of the modern world of capitalism, this part of the legal regulations is open and in favor of initial investment capital and its successful realization, and is constantly supplemented according to the need and function of capital growth in private equity or in balanced international law. All these "strictly defined rules" for the use of investment capital are dominated by its dictatorial, planned, and possessive centralized nature, without which it cannot survive. And without respecting its basic dictatorial characteristics, its users, creators, and protagonists of its realization cannot survive, to whom it is given as a means of initial fertilization and creative progress.

Financial capital is an unspent part of the planned and realized value of the past work of wage earners in the form of universal monetary value converted into a means of dominant capital that owns it and of which it is an integral part. This asset or money capital, like any other capital, has basically the dictated task of employing the labor and consumer function of a new number of wage earners or purchasing the means of production and other basic conditions that enable fruitful reproduction and creation of new accumulation of capital and financial profit. We recognize financial capital in other not only monetary pragmatic forms of capital placement, with the aim of making loan-sharking profits. This type of concentrated dictate of capital is also known in the course of earlier history. The sums of financial capital offered for use (borrowing and debt) are part of a strong monopoly and centralized position of planned accumulation and creation of dominant capital in social communities that are formed and subordinated in their emergence to the same goal by that same capital. Financial capital is always part of the cycle of creating past labor or current wage labor. Always on a daily and long-term basis, especially in recent history, it is legally refined to the maximum possible efficiency that it realizes through current creative human work of wage earners around the world. It is a consequence and expression of an independent nature and centralized control of capital, which demandingly grows from the capital itself formed into a sum of endless entrepreneurial alternatives which unfortunately belong in the nature of ownership and the right to manage to only a small part of the owners. Today, world financial capital is again monopoly and has more imperialist features than any other form of capital placement during the earlier history of capitalism. The financial capital of the developed countries of the world is a modern oligarch unrivaled by all the wage earners of the world. The instruments of its dictatorship and the capital relations in its daily realization are guaranteed by an extremely strong bureaucratic and military force that is unconditionally used in its realization when there are no other instruments of cooperation. Due to the dominance of capitalism as a world system, we most often speak and notice in everyday life the realization of the financial capital of the capitalist economy. However, let us recall that today, as is evident in the nature of China's financial capital around the world and earlier in the Eastern European block of socialist European countries, the financial and any other dominance of USSR capital over Warsaw Pact members and many other countries subordinate to it was noticeable. Precisely because of these experiential and contemporary facts, it can be concluded that both financial and every other form of dominant capital in world reproductions is a typical universal principle of realization of reproduction cycles of all revolutions and all worldviews grown from human creative history. If we analytically examine the emergence of dominant financial capital functions in the last sixty years and its share in world figures showing new profits and accumulation, we will see that the share of accumulations and profits of the financial sector in total profits of the world's most developed countries increased from 10-14% in the 1950s , to 45-60%, and even significantly more in today's total profit of the dominant capital of the most developed countries in the world, the so-called trillion dollars club of countries whose GDP exceeds one trillion dollars.

The division of the world defined in its basic features by the political, legal and economic systems of all countries of the world basically within that centralization of capital corresponds to the universal notion marked in everyday language and political jargon as *us* and *them*, our state and their state or nation, our allies and their allies, our comparative advantages in the economy in relation to their economic predispositions, our military force that protects us together with the alliance and their military force that threatens us... In this regard, in order to maintain their worldview dictated by dominant capital for these strategies of developed countries that own dominant capital, countless agents of their intelligence services cruise the world so that access to destruction, radical and tenacious opponents of the dominant world order can be prevented and destroyed. There is a vast unwritten reading in our everyday consciousness in which humanity is recognized within the regularly two opposite antipodes and the subordinate constantly frustrating features dictated by the capital and capital relation. There is no synthesis, there is only a planned trend of accumulation, capital, profit and capital relations in a known variant and a mathematically precise variant that is repeated for millennia. Our historical human being, which we unfortunately do not have at our disposal because it is constantly and immediately after birth formed by the dictates of capital, just like our life socialization, is only a part of the overall, given creative self-creation process to which we belong. Almost the absolute majority of the wage earners of the world and the population in general, always belong in their lives to the instruments of dictated and planned rules given to us by the dominant capital to which we belong in our social life as its creators in an infinite number of different forms of appearance within social reproductions. The present and modern self-creation of the human being through work is still not a permanent self-creative cycle of a free and functionally formed wage earner who has the right to decide with his universally harmonized attitudes on the whole value of his creative and self-creative work and its pragmatic social benefits.

Nevertheless, our daily companion is creative and self-creative work, and "a piece of the blue infinite UNIVERSE to which we belong primarily as freedom-creating beings" is always available with it.

Almost all possessive experiences prove that money can be converted as a universal means of exchange by an appropriate equivalent into any value. When it comes to financial capital with its planned centralized accumulation predispositions, its profits and accumulation are regularly and primarily secured under one condition, which is that the work and creativity of the wage population and its current work is ensured through the controlled market price of wage earners, a community in which it is always invested. The second most common condition is that the right to mortgage the real estate owned by the borrower exists and is secured. There are other forms of accumulation insurance that go beyond the current work of wage earners and enter deep into the sphere of other values of past material work that the debtor has at his disposal. The distance between the owner of the financial capital and the debtor who takes the loan is always defined by an open clause available to the owner of the financial capital which enables the owner of the financial capital to keep the debtor in the same position as the entire wage earners population around the world in a functionally growing standard of subsistence through the market price of labor determined by the planned financial part of the total centralized capital intended for the reproductive cycle and the payment of the function of the current labor of the wage earners of the world creating the accumulation of dominant capital. Let us recall the maxim about the rights and duties of wage earners.

The review of the operation of financial capital in its basic principles in the past sixty years will begin with a statement and catchphrase that has developed in the last sixty years as a fundamental motto in the basic almost dominant form of centralized financial capital around the world. Everyone has heard about the lesson: "what drill cannot do, money can". Rational understanding of this lesson is not difficult but not everyone has been able to use this lesson. In addition to other areas of use, teaching is certainly a daily motto related to profit and the processes of placement and creation of financial capital and profit in general, which is often an integral part of the dominant countries of the world with financial capital and trillion club members. The principles of borrowing and loansharking are basic in the lower strata of the owners of capital and capital relations. With the disappearance and condemnation of the imperialist wars, after the two world wars and many local wars still fought for freedom from the physical presence of imperial authorities in colonial countries around the world, the world has acquired new and much more elegant features of capital placement and capital relations by the greedy nature of dominant capital. We see this in new strategies that capital creates and provides secured capital, the relation of the conquered wage classes around the world uses and offers through dictated features of capital in the form of intellectual property, technical and technological licenses and other areas of advanced human creative work, most often from a wide scientific arsenal of not only local but also world scientists who have been bought, selected and incorporated for their needs by the developed dominant capital in their pragmatics through their patents for appropriate monetary or some other type of reward and compensation. These strategic dominant investment policies of the 1960s were joined to a much greater extent by the dominant world financial capital of the most developed countries of the world, which began to fertilize within rich and developed countries but also exported around the world under special conditions, especially to promising and underdeveloped countries which openly accepted all the offers of the financial sector of the dominant countries of the world, thinking that the work of their wage earners would succeed in creating new accumulation, capital and profit or repay huge debts cut by lending from world banks to which they were indebted. That did not happen, or very rarely did. The debts of these less developed countries of the world quadrupled very quickly due to the impossibility of repayment and the basic interest debt. There was no way out, so with the permission of the lender or financial capital, the refinancing of debts with additional refinancing, which means that additional funds and debts were defined due to "easier portions of repayment", or in moments of complete blockade and economic and financial collapse of debt corporations, the consent of the guarantors transferred their debts to their countries or turned them into public government debts. Along with the government debt, a mortgage and a clause in favor of the lender were obligatorily marked, which defined that if the state defaults on its government debts, the International Monetary Fund and its member providers of funds and loans have the right to collect receivables from the state. Debts were not repaid either, and the dominant financial capital embarked on debt restructuring programs, which is essential in this phase of defining a complete dictatorship and controlling the dominance of the legal, economic and po-litical system of indebted countries through debt as a condition that ensures its recovery from the value and on-going control of wage labor. The currencies of these countries, their money, and the entire banking system, in-cluding the central state banks, became part of the debt credit accounts overnight with a huge mortgage in the hands of the lender. It is quite certain that the dominant capital of the world planned the subordination of debt eco-nomic reproductions for a long time, even the complete collapse and re-assistance and restructuring of the legal, political and economic system of these communities, of course in its favor. The economic, legal and political col-lapse of the world's debt countries, directed by the owners of financial capital, at that stage, as a condition of debt survival, required complete restructuring of those coun-tries, which essentially means that these countries have gradually changed their political, legal and economic pro-file of relatively free countries into a new profile of completely subordinate hybrid communities of identical features of the legal political and economic system re-quired by role models and lenders who thus continued to ensure credit and controlled survival of these countries within the international world economic order. Restructuring usually brings new parts of the legal system that defines new taxes and payroll allocations in favor of the debtor's bureaucratic institutions so that the lender can repay the agreed portions of debts through monthly install-ments. Mass imitation and uncritical rewriting of legal acts and adaptation of new profiles from "successful role models" and experiences of the most developed countries in the world or areas where role models dominated according to the dictated demand of dominant capital, which is regularly the owner of financial capital, defined their complete subordination to monopoly imperialism and the empire of dominant capital that is constantly appearing on the world stage in new forms of financial capital. This was a logical sequence of the transition of small state and underdeveloped economies around the world from somewhat disparate and incompatible political legal and economic systems within their reproductive cycles to components of a global unified and centralized system controlled and developed through a centralized dominant capital function which controls by far the largest and most vital part of the world's financial capital. Consent to unconditional dictate and adoption of the dominance of more developed capital requires a completely different understanding of the creative sovereignty of less developed countries. For dominant capital, the value profile of debt states and nations receives a definite known monetary market value that can be disposed of regardless of political constraints. Likewise, from the perspective of current creative activity and the values of past and current work, smaller communities have become aware of their real daily values with which they can present themselves in the open world economic community they have adopted and to which they belong. Just to illustrate these claims with a just-published comparison in the world press that points out that in early 2019 the world's richest company Amazon outgrew (GDP = \$ 671 trillion) Swiss GDP of \$ 670 trillion. Amazon's GDP is projected to be $ 2 trillion in 2020, which is significantly more than Great Britain's GDP and many other countries in the world. Mr. Jeff Bezos, the owner of Amazon and the richest man in the world, at least at the moment, owns 116 billion dollars in personal ownership. If we compare Amazon and its owner Mr. Bezos with less developed countries whose GDP lacks 100 billion dollars, we would get a fantastic series or order of countries (or companies) that lag far behind the accumulated wealth of Amazon's owner and many other rich people in the world. This also points to the value order in at least one part of the world's dominant capital to which Amazon belongs. On the other hand, from Amazon's perspective, one can systematically dispose of accumulation and capital from past and current work, financial and intellectual capital and most importantly current wage labor that certainly multiplies existing investments and creates and maintains a hierarchy of dominance and concentration of capital according to the principle in which the legality "the greater the accumulation of value from wage labor, the greater the capital and profit" dominates, as well as its relentless direction and control of new reproductive cycles that enter both locally and at the level of the world economy in which it is present. The principle of capital growth around the world is the same, but its security and qualitative and quantitative characteristics are growing much faster in developed countries, which realize by far the largest accumulation of capital from wage labor and controlled growth of wage consumption of all kinds in their own community or around the world. The growth of the dominant amount of investment and operating capital in rich communities is growing much faster not only from domicile wage earners labor and investment in new capital accumulations but also global capital accumulation where free investment capital is increasingly present, even violently necessary. Just to repeat, intellectual capital and financial capital do not need a passport to be hosted in their functions in any part of the world. According to the latest data, the 26 richest people in the world have a far higher value of property than 3,800,000,000 billion people (Data from Davos 2019). Last year, 44 world richest people made up for the same population of the world. Does this indicate to us that the goals of the existing legal economic and political systems that define existing capital are subordinated to the interests of growth of accumulation of dominant capital through engaged and controlled creativity of world wage earners for those capital owners who are in the top zone on the scale of value ownership and make up for 0,1% (or much lower number) of the world population and essentially represent full compatibility with legal political and economic systems because these systems originated in their direction. Everything is subordinated to them and their controlled system of social reproduction. The rest of the non-owner wage earners or more modest owners of capital in these same reproductions and in the modern political legal and economic systems of the world, which are absolutely the largest part of this pragmatic functional creation, are in charge of submissive wage labor. The largest population of wage earners has constantly, during historical development and in radical bourgeois and socialist revolutions, had no significant influence on the political legal and economic system itself, which has never fundamentally changed the existing capital relation. Although all legal systems belong to the owners of capital and profit accumulation, they are regenerated in pragmatic procedural functions with the newly created accumulation, capital, and profit from wage earners labor of all strata and all tax brackets involved in reproduction. Legally protected instruments of growth and accumulation of capital and profit in the benefit of the owner of the dominant capital that arises in the constant process of wage creative and self-creative past and live current work is an extremely fluid process which currently depicts the entire pyramid of creators and its qualitative peak, and also the entire anatomy of humanistic creative civilization to which we belong and its given organization. Does this qualitative peak that legally possesses the accumulation, capital and profit of economic civilizational achievements indicate in its everyday functions that in the processes of change even the most vital parts of humanity who own dominant capital are also ready and responsible for the existing reality and future and for radical changes or, because they do not know (or may not want) better and more useful tools than the existing capital relation, and do not want any changes? The ignorance of humanity seems to be absolutely universal, and there is almost no difference in relation to the clear goals of change necessary for the revolutionary development of modern humanity between rich citizens and wage earners and those who are poor. The goal of both is always new capital, capital relation and accumulation of capital from other people's wage labor that they want to own for their own benefit. Independent dominant capital very often bypasses the parliamentary democratic bodies of modern states in which interests and intentions of poorer wage earners and citizens are presented via delegates.

In tax brackets of both corporations and citizens, the anatomy and blood flow of each capital relation within all types of reproductive relations is shown in the most vivid way. We will deal with this anatomy later in order to bring the relationship between capital of capital less workers and workers possessing capital as subjects of reproductive systems even closer to the focus of the reader.

Taxation of large corporations is minimal, and in relation to the regular taxation of wage earners and citizens it is a ridiculously low amount. We must not forget that the laws that define taxes and tax brackets are the legal product of the democratic consciousness of member of parliaments intoxicated and subordinated to the dominant capital and capital relations of the modern communities of the world. In the election procedures for the functional positions of modern governments and parliamentary bodies, the exclusive interest of protection and legal development of the dominant capital and its accumulation prevails. Almost all delegates to congresses and senates in the United States, as well as representatives in parliaments and governments of the most developed countries in the world, regardless of their political current, take their oaths aware that their primary goal is legal protection and development of capital and capital relations of their country in relation to the environment of the world. And the authorized governments and prime ministers of these governments want almost no restrictions in their work of representing and placing the dominant capital of these communities. Everything is subject to the dictates of capital that form them into arbitrary dictators who often extreme usurp power into their own hands. There is an impression that many modern world parliamentary systems have not moved far from the dictatorial Roman practice in which an extreme dictator with a lyre at hand in the Nero ecstasy of an omnipotent, intellectually blind man can burn down a modern, much larger megalopolis in order to change and destroy ballast beings on the way to the gods.

MORE ABOUT FINANCIAL CAPITAL

All banks of local or wider major and more extensive financial significance that deal with lending to various programs of citizens are built on identical principles as the mega-financial institutions of the world that enable them. The further away they are in a compatible and dictated range from the central bank capital and official policies of dominant political parties, they are more aggressive and more focused on the accumulation and creation of frequent and rigorously defined bank loans with mortgages that repay their function of lending to the central bank or dominant capital and capital ratio, based on significantly higher interest income than borrowing from central banks of state and federal institutions or the assistance of the world banking system. The savings of citizens and wage earners do not exist today because there is no interest on savings. The reason for this is primarily in the redirection of any amount of money from a static to an active role, of course always under control and in favor of the bearer and subject of the dictates of dominant financial capital. The growth of bank profits is constantly ongoing while the growth of wage earnings and savings is stagnating. Interest on bank savings has completely disappeared from banking operations with citizens in the past 30 years. Citizens' savings have been redirected to investment funds and the stock market, which most citizens do not use due to ignorance of the functionality of this type of economy or due to possession of small amounts of money that citizens and wage holders have deposited in these banks. Thus, the active benefits and predispositions of their small funds in the stock market and other funds were taken over by banking institutions in which these modest but associated wage sums of money generate decent bank profits. A citizen is creditworthy only if he shows that the bank has the right to a mortgage on some of the value that the citizen owns, most often real estate, or if he proves that his earnings and current work not only in one job but often doing two or three jobs, can return monthly portions of his debt if he needs credit. If these conditions are not determined by the lender in the financial institution, the loan cannot be realized. Loans that are realized have within the monthly repayment specified interest and interest agreed profit for the lender, that are adjusted according to the dictates of the money market, which the lender imposes after five-year, seven-year, ten-year, twenty-year or longer loan repayment periods. Furthermore, you are no longer entitled to early loan repayment if you do not pay the repayment penalty before the expiration of the time provided for the duration of your loan obligations, which rises to 10% of the debt, which is often part of the citizen's contract with the lender, especially for the first part of the repayment term (5-7 years). This is another typical conditional dictate and attack on the freedom of civil rights in the free financial market. All terms and conditions of debt repayment in each credit relation are primarily subordinated to the interests of financial capital controlled by central state banks by issuing cheap money on the market and within the functions of smaller banks, which through lending and increased interest in the new debt ratio often make a triple profit in relation to principal debt in all parts of the reproduction system, both in the business of wage earners and in production corporations and in the widest consumption. The cycles of borrowing and debt repayment do not stop, but financial capital is constantly increasing along with the projected accumulation and its growth of a geometric nature, as well as the growth of capital of corporations in which they enter, which ensures primarily wage work of corporations in the reproduction cycle. The entire duration of the financial capital cycle from the moment of loan to the realization of profit is not possible without wage labor that generates newly created value and is an integral part of the planned loan calculation which becomes a rigorous law that dictates the overall behavior of all participants in the time process of fertilization of financial capital. The link between financial institutions and private capital, which realizes almost all other forms of accumulation of newly created capital from wage labor, is unbreakable. This extremely important link that ensures the vitality of each reproductive cycle is marked and defined primarily by a pragmatic legal system that is constantly being written down for this purpose. And from the perspective of modern loan-sharking financial capital, not everything is perfectly defined, especially if the consumer abilities of wage earners and their long-term debt predisposition are not foreseen, which is far more often a consequence of uncoordinated macro-reproductive relations in the entire economic cycle. In such situations, wage labor often cannot be self-sustaining, as was the case in the Great Depression of 2008, in which the enormous solan-sharking bank capital and wage society standard in the USA suffered.

Dominant capital is formally divided and not in one place. It is located mainly within the economies of the most developed countries in the world or in joint financial and strategic institutions and agencies of special interest for the survival and development of dominant capital around the world. The global appearance of dominant capital and financial capital belonging to it in the world reproductive economy is united by a strategy of common principal features of capital that are highly respected in the daily actions of businessmen around the world until a new unknown or created form of crisis capital directs them towards different, often extremely conflicting actions and behaviors.

VARIATIONS OF USE FUNCTIONS OF CAPITAL

Each form of materialized past labor is a strategic value and a component of dominant capital, protected by the legal system, most often in the form of private ownership. In particular, security activities are highlighted in those areas that are the result of the latest and extremely pragmatic ongoing creative work that guarantees an increase in particular capital and its accumulation. The complex and specialized information systems of different countries of corporations, companies, groups, or individuals are the most prominent strategic areas in the antagonistic world of capital and capital relations of the modern world that we encounter in recent times. Huge memories of strategic data are invaluable to the communities that own them and never, at least in recent history, even though they are of general importance to all mankind, do they belong to that same humanity as freely available elements of the creative work of all creators. Information is the capital and its availability are as distributed as the distribution and control of capital holdings. Information systems are integrated into a huge memory market. The way these memories are formed, and the availability and benefits of information systems regularly define the capital that created them. The greater the dominance of capital, the greater its intention to create autarchic information systems that belong only to the owners of capital. Just as the state communities of the world are lined up in the world reproduction pyramid, according to the strength of their dominant capital, the information systems of these countries are part of a strategic orientation and a tool of self-domination that guarantees the creation of new accumulation and capital. Ordinary wage earners and citizens are most often provided with operational daily information for a fee that enables them to function more efficiently in their daily wage life in which they make their own profit or accumulation in accordance with the reproductive cycles of production and consumption controlled by dominant capital. Information is, just as much as information systems and the memories that belong to them, a part of the total past and live current work of all mankind as well as any capital or newly created value. Even in their growth into the most modern information assemblies, information systems have used their function throughout history and today they use it as a strategic function of capital relations and the creation of capital accumulation. The means and tools we use today to make vital parts of the information system available to us tend to indicate that they transfer every part of human immanent memory into vast systems that in time and space become an integral part of vast memories available only for a fee. There is no choice, the whole of humanity is subject to tendentious tools and external protected memory is available only through the controlled mediation of capital. The most efficient form of access to information, both those from the deepest of one's own intimacy and those in the most remote reaches of human past work, is available only for a fee. Very often we find our own information that we have stored in the memory resources offered to us for this purpose in a completely different order and coordination than we have formed it. The strategic systems of the modern capitalist and socialist communities of the world that serve the dominant capital are numerous and often inaccessible to the majority of the wage and bourgeois population, even with compensation. The hierarchy and pyramid of capital that is so typical of the modern cross-section and presentation of the possessions of the values of past work and live current work of the world's workers is applicative and illustrative to show the functions and availability of modern information systems that are its parallel ally and companion.

LONG-TERM DEBT STRATEGY

Divided coexistence or survival of formal alliances of dominant capital of different developed and mutually tolerant communities of the world is possible today as it was possible in the previous history of human labor for the simple reason that still, especially from the perspective of dominant capital and progressive creativity of these countries, there is a market of all forms of capital and of course the need for investments around the flower that is calculated, stimulated and maintained from the centers of power of dominant capital as an essential condition for survival and maintenance of a growing controlled constant of accumulation, capital and profit. Dominant capital regularly appears in each new cycle with new forms and new means of capital placement from the wide and coquettish arsenal of financial capital, innovations and technical-technological licenses, information monopoly and information systems of various strategic memories and many other means that are applied to legal political and economic systems around the world. All this is unified by international law which guarantees the dominant function of capital relations in favor of dominant capital and its owners. Extremely aggressive dynamics of new forms of imperial capital relations began again in the early 1960s all around the world including domination over their own wage earners population. Debts in the form of loans that are returned in monthly portion from wage labor are also a guaranteed profit. Debts in the USA, GB, Germany, China, and other developed countries are also the largest debts of today's world economy simply because they are formed by the largest population of wage earners employed or controlled by the capital of these countries and world. The goal of any economic power is to create a centralized polycentric accumulation and control of capital in the hands of a small number of owners of dominant capital that controls part or all of the world's economic reproduction and most importantly the accumulation of capital from wage labor in favor of a small number of private owners or bureaucratic and political institutions, such as the case in China. For this purpose, all wage labor around the world is very aggressively subordinated by dominant capital through unified legal systems to the unconditional growth of accumulation and growth of total dominant capital created without distinction by those wage earners of small underdeveloped countries and wage earners in the most develop countries of the world. The modern world is becoming more and more unitary and controlled wage cage dictated by the abstract dictates of the existing amount of dominant capital created by the past creative and self-creative work of wage earners and its conditional account of geometric progression given as a constant reproductive obligation to few systems of the world that are in its service (rule of law). If we accept the thesis that there is no part of the newly created accumulation of capital which is not created by human past or current creative work, it can simply be concluded that the development of imperial or world monopoly on accumulation, capital and profit by the owner of the dominant capital has led to the achievement of the conditions for at least two basic characteristics of capital as an abstract target value that is constantly anticipated as an available reality but also as an economic goal of the owner of capital, which are: first, control of the flows of accumulation, capital, and profit in general in social reproductions, and second, control of the social and productive functions and potentials of its creators - the wage earners of the world in reproductive cycles. The processes that keep these two functions of capital in use are present everywhere in the world wherever dominant capital is present. There is no place for any other pragmatic practice, nor does it exist, so it is important to understand and anticipate that the nature of the dictates of capital and capital relations will necessarily be our companion in the near future. Regardless of the fact that there is a privileged hierarchical layering or scale of beneficiaries in the realized practice and profile of existing capital and capital relations with the basic whose creation of dominant capital, starting from the owner of dominant capital at the top of social scales and the lowest rewarded wage earner for his wage function, this system fulfills its historical role by alimenting each of its layers. However, it is not static and eternal and is subject to constant pragmatic changes. This basic goal, which determines the creation of primarily accumulation, capital and profit, is in principle a given goal and is regularly the result of the tight skin of total constantly expanding capital within the rule of law given to every living being, corporation or political community. The reality of the distribution of accumulation, capital and profit is the pragmatic legality (not a general principle based on moral and scientific laws) of appropriated (stolen) rights over the past and current work of wage earners both during historical development and today, which, with the growth of the creative and self-creative wage earning role in the modern world and socio-economic functions and reproduction, will change significantly in the future to come.

The historical evolutionary genesis of the human species knows no other values than those values that arise from live current human labor. These values in the dialectical cycle have constantly defined in an expanding contrast each degree of both earlier human creativity, which we call the values of past work, and the currents of modern work. Our historical being will be essentially defined forms both for our lives by our own current work and the live current work of the wage earners who are our contemporaries and parallel creators. In order to better understand the message of this statement, we must know that past work is constantly present in the forms of realized material and intellectual values, while live current work as the foundation of the current reproductive process is based on adopted values of past work and contemporary creativity and self-creativity enabled by the legal functions of the dictatorship of capital. Both past and live current work are the only known capital that we have realized and accumulated through our work and creativity. It is for this reason that the well-known civilization capital, whether we own it or not, is our singular, particular, and universal primary interest. Our motive directed towards the possession of these values that define us in our present cosmic movement is primarily marked by creative self-awareness and an understanding of its social functions. Our socialization and consciousness are constantly obsessed with the capital of civilization as it is offered in the flow of all values and constantly directs us to appropriate those values that enable us. For this reason, our daily creative and self-creative activity is primarily focused on the appropriation of accumulation, capital, and profit from our own and wage labor, because other values do not exist or are created in some other way without human creative work. Two types of appropriation of the value of human labor are historically known: a primitive or primary collection of the value of human labor of shorter duration without the accumulation of capital or surpluses of human creative labor. What is not expended in these primary creative stages of development is the conscious creative and self-creative potential memory and energy that directs us to new higher goals. While the second recognizable form of appropriation of the value of human labor is actually conceived on the basis of creative human labor and its organization which creates not only minimal sums of value intended for short-term consumption but also surpluses of value which are both the first forms of created capital and also the first forms of new, yet unseen capital relations which in various processes throughout history have enabled the emergence of innumerable and diverse forms of capital dominance and its historical role that continues to this day. At this stage, creative and self-creative work is the source of all the memorized values, both those we consume and those that the protagonists of capital relations and wage labor appropriate to their advantage through the legal system and use as investment capital.

The procedures of appropriating the value of surplus past labor and the value of live current labor during our historical genesis have stratified users and owners of total values of past labor in the forms of newly created material values, as well as the possession of memory of well-known creativity. Stratification of the protagonists of creative current work into wage earners, creators of newly created value who, since they are not holders of previous surpluses of equity, were kept at the level of the primary consumption reward, although the value of their work significantly exceeded those values, and members of the second basic layer of wage earners, also creators, to whom, with the help of legal systems (which developed in parallel within the needs of this layer of wage earners) and with the development of surpluses and unspent values, full control of surpluses (capital accumulation, profits) and past wage labor was available, as well as current wage labor and society as a whole. This social stratification that controls the absolute majority of creators and self-creators of accumulation, capital and profit is identical today in its profile to its earlier models and represents the primary interest of the capitalist economy of the modern world without which capitalism and modern socialism could not survive.

The antagonism among the members of the dominant trillion club has recently become more pronounced, especially in the strategy that defines the control of the wage population of the world, both its quantitative and qualitative part and characteristics. In particular, this antagonism and strategy of dominant capital is noticeable in the relationship between dominant capital and the most numerous wage-earning populations of China and India. In order for the dominant capital to grow, this huge population of wage earners is necessary both as dictated cheap creators but also as dictated consumers of newly created use values and users of accumulation and capital from their own work managed by oligarchs of trillion dollars club members, and also the domestic oligarchs of those communities that are constantly being formed. It was noted that in 2019, China formed and enabled the emergence of the largest number of millionaires in the world. What is almost impossible to constantly control by the dominant capital is the accelerated development and accumulation that these most numerous wage earning countries have in the creative potential of their market-cheap wage earning population which in its creative and self-creative being manages to create "its own domestic amount of accumulation, capital and profit" in addition to the debt amount of accumulation and new capital belonging to investors, holders of dominant capital from countries that use this wage population for their own goals. What the Chinese experience shows is the extremely fast growth of the GDP of that country whose soon dominance (together with the Indian population) will be the new face of world capital and accumulation around the world. This new face of accumulation and capital, although not far removed from the traditional rules of use of capital instruments and capital relations, will significantly raise the level of availability of new, richer accumulation and newly created capital to many wage earners in China, India and other countries around the world which is also its only creator in the current work of reproductions of these countries. The legitimacy of dialectical growth and accelerated development of creators, based on the creative work of the wage population, which in Chinese practice of the 20th and 21st centuries is recognized as the transition from quantity to new quality, is a solid guide to the future which we have already stated that gradually but surely provides the wage population with the right to dispose of an increasing part of the accumulation but also the growing presence of wage earners in the creative and self-creative process that allows new and significantly changed worldview and power. This share of holdings of accumulation and capital will constantly grow in favor of the wage earners of the world and not only in Chinese practice but also in other countries of the world in accordance with the dynamics and intensity of reproductive processes. What we still see in the example of the wide range of Chinese development and

Chinese creative currents, including its stagnation and intensive development, is its growing influence on world socioeconomic reproductions. The presence of the now international Chinese economy, rich in domestic and foreign financial capital, licenses and technical-technological products and the rhythm of the most developed countries in the world, significantly affects the world flows of accumulation and capital in both positive and negative terms. The old rules and procedures for curbing and controlling accumulative growth and capital used in the second half of the 20th century and the beginning of the 21st century in monopoly imperialism and financial subordination of countries by debt by developed countries and their financial capital will have to change significantly in the future (new rules have probably already been prepared) precisely because of the experiences of the world economy in Chinese practice. The rules of international democratic cooperation have a constantly new legal form regardless of ideological differences and political profile of countries participating in the world reproductive system, which is dictated by world dominant capital and capital relations as a constantly new strategic culture of creativity of all participants in world reproductive trends, which has already become a common practice today. One thing is for sure, and that is that the huge potential of quantum and quality of a large population of wage earners from China, India and other countries will not be dropped from the primary orientations and interests of the most vital visions of powerful capital owners from the trillion club countries but also from the hands and control of Chinese, Indian and other "domestic" owners of accumulation and investment capital. An equally parallel process of world dominant capital in conquering and exercising the functions of wage earners in future world reproductions will certainly enable an increasing part of accumulation and capital to belong to that part of the wage population which has not owned it so far or has owned it in minimum necessary quantities only in the form of minimum wages that ensured survival. Gandhi's vision of revolution and the participation of Indian wage earners in parts of accumulated capital will certainly be gradually woven into the common goals of both Indian and world capital. The traditional legality of legal systems that has defined wage labor in these countries will be enriched by new principled ethical maxims of a universally creative human being who will be realized in the far near future than is usually seen. Billions of new wage earners, with new qualitative characteristics, will be included in the world processes of production and consumption, which is also a new form of revolution that will significantly emphasize the new quantitative and qualitative conditions of reproductive cycles and the dynamics of their changes. However, just to emphasize that all this will happen gradually and in possible controlled forms, the dictatorship of capital and capital relations as we know them today, regardless of who owns them, because humanity has no other form of socio-economic relations nor is it known to prepare and create them for future use. It is undeniable that the power of wage earners has grown during the 19th, 20th and 21st centuries and is present but still the wage earners of the world are no other revolutionary being who can change the world into an economic system without capital and capital relations, even if they wanted to. Therefore, even in the near future, there will be no significant radical revolutionary changes in the legal creative culture of wage earners and the world's population. The lesson to the owners of world dominant capital that has been gained in the case of the development of the Chinese economy can be formulated in the following sentence: as much as it is controlled by its owners and legal oligarchic world institutions, fertilization of capital is what we can see wage labor, its quantity and quality are legal and the only source not only of new profits and accumulation of world capital invested in China, but also of extremely rapid and efficient development of capital accumulation of Chinese hybrid capitalist socialist corporations controlled by the Chinese Communist Party bureaucracy. This growth of the Chinese economy based on numerous and hard-working and market-cheap Chinese wage earners in the past 40 years has created a new China but also a new world economic order in which there is a new quality of dominant capital belonging to a new economic superpower created by cheap Chinese wage earners. The emergence and growth of the Chinese economy from complete misery to the level of the second economic power in the world with a GDP of 15 trillion dollars was created in just forty years. The world's accumulation of capital and profit stake are divided significantly differently today than they were 40 years ago. If the identical trend of investment by world dominant capital continues, which is an almost inevitable solution to the globalization of world capital into India's even larger wage population, it is to be expected that the same scenario will occur and that the country will have similar results as China. The question imposed to the owners of investment capital intended for India is whether it is possible to control the growth and development of mass wage populations at the level of balanced tolerant pragmatic mutual economy or whether, as in the case of China, and if the development of the Indian subcontinent will soon grow into a new independent world force as it is the case in China. India is already the world's fourth largest economic power, as self-sufficient and strategically independent as China. The future of the world's investment capital, but also the future of states and communities with a wage population of one or two billion (in the case of China and India combined, two billion wage population) of potential wage earners and consumers, is essentially inseparable from the relatively new form of globalization of dominant capital, which can be seen in the constant political and economic agitation and action of the representatives of these countries who prepare and supplement the whole process on a daily basis. Let me remind you of the theses of the previous text dominant capital at the same time socialize the culture of economics which is based on the dictates of capital and capital relations. This new quantitative and qualitative addition to the modern developed capitalism of the world is an important basis and guarantee of new cycles of the capitalist reproductive economy in the future as well. Most world wage earners do not know other than capitalism other social relations and organization of social communities. Theses on the implementation of the ideas of global communism that dominated the 19th and 20th centuries or a new communist manifesto in the modern world that offers a solution has no real basis because it is completely unknown to the modern population of wage earners both as a theoretical model and as a pragmatic practice. Moreover, in the not-so-distant past 30 years ago, all European socialist communities, including Yugoslav self-governing socialism, which showed remarkable initial results, were rejected, and turned into capitalism by a referendum of wage earners, resembling a successful Western civilization model. Communism, however, is not lost and rejected as a worldview and as a model of humanity, as it will be constantly present to a greater or lesser extent in modern capitalism that created it and still creates it in modern political and socio-economic trends of the world's most developed societies and the distant future. There is plenty of evidence for that in the USA, England, Germany, France, Denmark, Spain, and many other countries around the world. Probably the most interesting and extensive movement of the socialist-communist population is expressed in its active presence in the democratic election campaign of the Democratic Party of the United States of America, where a commitment to millions to socialism and communism programs is noticeable, especially among young and educated, which has been offered by the Democratic Party veteran Bernie Sanders in his program for 20 years, both as a senator but also in the candidacy procedures for the position of the President of the USA. Despite all the outstanding results in the 2019 and 2020 election process shown by Bernie Sanders'' program, the majority conservative current of the Democratic Party of the USA that distanced itself from socialism and communism represented by former US Vice President Joe Biden still completely eliminated Bernie Sanders' socialist communist platform that was offered to American citizens and of course him as a candidate for president of the USA in the 2020 general elections.

Traditional dominance and complete control by dominant capital, the reproductive cycles of the world, each of its layers and each function is recognizable both in time and space all around us. Unfortunately, the majority of the world's population is completely ignorant and uneducated in that it could understand the whole system of subordination to the dictates of dominant capital in the hands of a small group, world oligarchs and capital owners who are completely unknown to them. The world as we know it is far more like an evolutionary anthill than the free creation of a creative rational human being. The practice of capital and capital relations is still the only pragmatic means and criterion of the useful that belongs to the modern human homo sapiens of recent times, regardless of what has been judged on it. The causes of this situation are primarily in the use of the dictatorship of capital and capital relations as the basic tools and sense of human existence created in the early history of human creativity, which is embraced in the conditionally modeled ignorant population of citizens of all generations today. All the policies and ideologies that we know and for which both wage earners and wage earning owners of capital as well as all other

engaged population of the world have opted in their political traces in the historical history so far have aimed at
changing or modifying the management of capital and
newly created value in reproductive cycles, capital and
capital relations. These principled determinants of earlier
history, the present, and the intention of the future are eternally throughout history the subject of revolutions of the
most varied ideological charge. This task of eliminating
capital, the relationship between its exploitative origins of
accumulation and capital, no matter how much it is present
in countless resolutions of different ideologies, has never
been changed in real society and worldview of world communities. The only changes that we can follow throughout
history as quantitative and qualitative progress of mankind
are traces of constant creative wage creative and self-
creative work woven into the value of materialized past
human work and current work of modern generations of
wage earners managed by owners and managers of capital
using the inevitable dictatorship of capital as a categorically rational alibi of the creative existence of humanity.

As long as there is creative human labor of the world's
wage earners as an integral part of the dictates of dominant
capital in both private and social or non-proprietary rela-
tionships where its dictatorial function turns into a rational
creative mission, there will be hope for quantitative and
qualitative change and understanding of the universe in a
new way. In the processes of creation, the wage earners of
the world (wage earners with and without capital) and the
whole of humanity increasingly follow the rational reason

for creative goals and will be less and less under the control and dictates of private capital and capital relations. Contemporary creativity of world wage earners serves to create superior values of capital, as the goal of future successful creative social communities is to create a versatile creative and self-creative human being that will not be subordinated to the creation of any value unless it has primarily social accessibility and its rational profile available to every citizen.

What is evident for now is that both earlier and present but also future history has enabled the continuity of human creative work generated by the symbiosis of universal movement of matter and creative work of self-conscious wage earners of owners and non-owners of dominant capital and the legal dictates of capital and its capital relations. This symbiosis, which is reflected in creative work, has always and unconditionally, both during earlier history and today, made it possible to break through the layer of the existing dictatorship of capital that created its enlargement in the hands of a small number of capital owners. What we call the layer of dictatorship of dominant capital or any capital is the quantified and qualified range of organized values and memory of past material labor and live current labor of wage earners expressed in the generally known amount of capital in social relations of production and creation planned from (as) guaranteed surplus value of wage labor. The layer of the dictatorship of known capital always and regularly plans a known sum of surplus value, accumulation and emergence of new capital, which arises exclusively by using the value of past materialized human labor in the creative processes of live current work of world wage earners.

GROWTH OF CAPITAL DICTATE CONSTANT

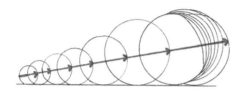

The parallel growth of the dictatorship of capital with creative and self- creative work in both regular and irregular elliptical forms are always fulfilled and defined by the dictate of capital.

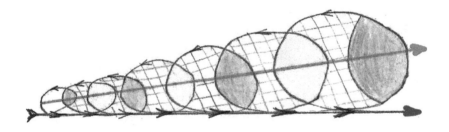

Attachments 1 and 2. The parallel development of human creative and self-creative work and the dictatorship of capital that accumulates new values of human creative work in the sum of new operating capital essentially reflects the present amount of materialized past work and live current work in time and space.

Illustration explanation: a display of three separate, yet inseparable parts of historical cycles in an endless string in the form of a growing spiral of creative and self-created work and newly created values in which the red represents the values of past work brought into the new cycle, the mesh space is the expenditure of new creative and self-creative work in the process of a new cycle, while the green represents the accumulation of new value (profit or new operating capital for the next cycle). All three parts of the "spiral movement" are in constant expansion defined by both individual and total average radius marked by a red arrow that represents constant growth in the process of relatively independent capital dictatorship, which is present in each part of the ever-increasing radius of the spiral that vividly epitomizes human history. EXPANSION AND GROWTH OF MATERIALIZED VALUES OF PAST WORK, LIVE CURRENT WORK AND CAPITAL ACCUMULATION HAVE THE TENDENCY OF FULL SYMBIOSIS AND CONCORDANCE WITHIN THE GROWING RADIUS OF THE HISTORICAL SPIRAL OF CREATIVE HUMAN WORK, WHICH WILL CHANGE OVER TIME AND THUS ELIMINATE THE EXISTING LEGAL ECONOMIC AND POLITICAL SYSTEMS THAT NURTURE THE DICTATORSHIP OF PRIVATE OR BUREAUCRACY CAPITAL AND CAPITAL RELATIONS. The overlap and identification of the quantity and quality of past human work as created material basic reproductive conditions of new reproductions and live current work at some stage of development will eliminate the capital and capital re-lation as a private or social possession. Then, creative human work unencumbered by the possession of capital will become a universal permanent free creative force, compatible exclusively with the achieved degree of un-derstanding and possession of the freedom of universal movement which will constantly grow with creative human work to the infinity of the universe. The future creative human work as well as the basic materialized human work will be much more defined by the scientific understanding of the universe and the universal move-ment, which we are an integral part of on this planet, and not by private ownership and pragmatics of capital and capital relations. The reason for this is primarily the scientific constants and the compatibility of current hu-man creative work with universal laws, without which it is impossible to expect any significant (not just ex-perimental) step into the vastness of the universe. The existing degree of cohesion of objective scientific re-search aimed at understanding the enduring peculiarities of universal laws and, in this regard, the relation to hu-man creativity and modern capital and capital relations, is unfortunately still pragmatically selective in favor of accumulation of both capital and private property. In this selective peculiarity, protected by legal systems that are not necessarily scientific or generally principled moral determinants of contemporary creative and self-creative history, the pragmatics of capital as an external force and dictatorship dominates.

THE LAYER OF CAPITAL DICTATORSHIP

The growth and accumulation of the value of both completed materialized past labor and live current labor forms the relative sum of the total values at our disposal. This sum of values, whether viewed as part of a singular, particular or joint ownership of one person or corporation, state or all of humanity, becomes the reach of both current and potential values that are constantly taken into account in legality and processes of capital relations. The layer of the dictatorship of capital in the social relation of production constantly conditions growth towards greater and more comprehensive values. In order to achieve this growth, all known socio-political systems that used the capital relation (and others do not even exist) regularly engaged human creative current work of all wage earners, which is the only known means to meet the task of creating, breaking through and increasing existing capital.

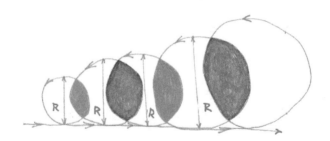

R-radius or layer of dominant capital in constant expansion
Live current work in expansion
Past work in expansion

Attachment 3: The whole of the historical currents of living and materialized human work can be observed in spiral cycles that represent years, centuries, millennia, but also the infinite temporal dimension in space and time. Contemporary historical trends are constantly growing and are recognizable in constantly new and comprehensive quantitative and qualitative features thanks mostly to the creative and self-creative past and live current human wage labor. Each new cycle is larger and more fruitful as we adopt it as a basic feature of our socialization and overall social and work participation. The dictates of capital have completely filled every human being and marked him as a value or as part of social relations of different values and calculations in processes in which each human being is present in different forms of creative and social participation. This verified potential calculation that everyone has at their disposal and self-awareness of self-worth, whether the fruit of one's own or offered assessment in social flows, also defines us as a usable part of the reproductive cycle of the whole society or the whole humanity, but also of the universal movement. Human creative and self-creative history does not record any event that is not covered by the dictatorship of capital. Essentially outside the dictates of capital and human wage creation and self-creation, which through the constant accumulation of capital elements the dictates of capital in the time and space at their disposal and marks the previous human history, nothing else is relevant and does not exist. At the modern stage of its development, humanity is not able to voluntarily abolish the dictates of capital. With the disappearance of the dictatorship of capital and capital relations, the entire civilizational culture created by human creative work for millennia and recorded in materialized past human labor and capital different economic quantitative and qualitative forms of civilizational cultures. The basic feature by which socializations form the historical being of man are primarily formed solid or fluid worldviews of our own creative value with which we belong to a broader and, of course, universal system of use values. These use values created by human labor are the basis of capital and capital relations in the process of creating new values of accumulation and new capital.

The spiral cycle of growth of creative wage and self-creative work of wage workers at the disposal of the dictatorship of capital can be presented as a linear geometric sum and growth of values dominated by geometric progression of capital and profit accumulation in favor of private and social owners of capital which are made possible by legal systems based on the created values of wage labor. Capital accumulation is the potential value of social communities and its legal owners as smaller groups of people who possess various forms of potential capital including possession and the right to dispose of the quantity and quality of creative current wage labor become responsible for the overall realization of the potential that capital accumulation potentially offers and of course dictates in the characteristics of the dictatorship of capital and capital relations. Basically, I primarily consider the development of creative and self-creative work in the sphere of reproductive cycles of material production, but also in all other parallel activities produced and conditioned by the dictates of capital and symbiosis of creative and self-creative work for the needs of increased reproduction.

Attachment 4: A pictorial representation given in a spiral representation of the growth of the process of creative and self-creative work, which in reality we find in the form of the value of past work (red color) and live current work (green color). These are at the same time the minimum and basic forms and variations of capital and its legally given accumulation values that enable this process of spiral increase.

All parts of the spiral cycles in their processes are defined by the "invisible layer of the dictatorship of dominant capital" which grows along with the growth of the value of human current and past creative work that forms it. It is important to note that the form of spiral magnification that we can follow throughout history following the proposed analogy of this Attachment is not formed by capital values in the form of static only potential materialized past labor ,but is formed exclusively by live current work of creators and self-creators. If the interventions of live current work disappeared from the spiral relation in which we observe the values of past work and live

current creative work, the whole system of values of past work would disappear into some other properties in the processes and laws of motion of the universe. In the spiral movement, the static states of the red and green phases, which represent the properties of materialized past and live current work, do not exist. The relationship between past materialized human creative work and live current work is constant and is primarily part of total cosmic movements in which the creative and self-creative processes of human work are compatible with the macrocosmic laws of motion of the universe, otherwise without this fundamental elements they could not exist. In the infinite number of the most rational human creative processes of creation and self-creation, not a single moment and not a single movement, conscious or not, exists without macrocosmic laws woven into it.

Attachment: 5 The Milky Way is our homeland in the orbit of one of the bright stars, and is just one of countless galaxies of the universe with countless spiral shapes, rhythms and deviations from rectilinear motion known in creative and self-creative consciousness as the natural geometric form of Heraclitus or Epicurus' philosophy, and in dialectics as a phenomenon of the transition of quantity into a new quality, or as an ordinary and frequent lesson in the jargon of everyday language for a partner and for his unsuccessful action which we characterize as "spinning in a circle" which we do not approve because we expect deviation, advancement towards new values and many other features that we often find in inductive descriptions as a deviation from a rectilinear or regular circular or rectilinear motion that leads us to new discoveries and creations. It is this deviation in the spiral motion of matter that represents the infinitely compatible realm of all universal alternatives to human creative and self-creative work and is the essential basis of its current and future creative and self-creative freedom without the dictates of capital and capital relations. The degree of our rational reach and understanding of the universe was illustrated by the famous theoretical physicist Dr. Neil deGrasse Tyson with the sentence: "perhaps cosmic beings do not want to communicate with terrestrial beings because we do not show a high enough degree of rational understanding of the universe." In the everyday worldly understanding of the differences between developed and underdeveloped humanity, we encounter the same difficulties and the impossibility of appropriate behavior and cooperation in all fields, not only in the basic features of the legality of productive and consumer cultures but also in religion, art, morals, philosophy and other areas of human action. Gradual consumption of the most perfect products of human creative work, modern most developed cultures of the world in underdeveloped economic communities must be well prepared to be realized in creative consumption, or otherwise it makes no sense.

An increasing and comprehensive understanding of the universe will enable human creative and self-creative practice to be more creatively independent of the dictates of capital. In these new processes, the basic features of the life and creative work of wage earners and self-creators will be the advanced rational creation of new values, and of course capital, but not capital as the capital relations or dictates of private property. The capital relation will inevitably grow into a non-proprietary social relation as well as the immanent rights to work and dispose of materialized past labor and live current labor. We will try to illustrate this by re-interpreting part of the process within the spiral movement (Attachment 5) of our creative and self-creative history generated by creative work in which the dictatorship of private capital is still present as the initiator and planner of creative and self-creative work of all currents and all wage strata, of both earlier and modern history.

Attachment: 6,

Creative and self-creative work in alternating phases of capital development as materialized past labor and also

138

as capital of live current labor of the world's wage earners, bounded by the veil layer and current reach of the dictatorship of capital (purple).

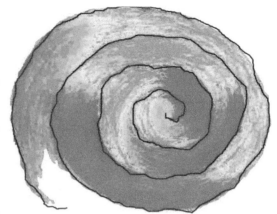

We have already pointed out that all historical development is under the control of the dictates of privately owned capital. We have emphasized the importance and role of creative and self-creative work of world wage earners throughout human history who bring to the historical scene new and quantitative and qualitative sums of values created by their work which in the forms of materialized work and livecurrent work become new quantitative and qualitative new imperative dictators. These potential sums of new values, in addition to the part of the value allocated for consumption and depreciation of production assets, become the basis of new reproduction plans in the characteristics and values of past work that is potential in its values but not recognizably current. Without wage current creative work which is the creative unifier of functional and pragmatic memories of all past work of earlier stages of creation in the form of potential capital and current creative and self-creative activities undertaken by current wage workers to create new accumulative value intended for new reproductive cycles, these values would not arise. In all cycles during the historical development of human creative and self-creative work there is a "legal democratically voted dictatorship of capital" which with its layer (Attachment: 7 purple) successfully controls the growth of almost all creative and self-creative reproduction and working history of mankind. We must emphasize in this part of the text that no matter how powerful and legally authorized capital is, it is not always possible to master and fully subordinate to its goals the creative and self-creative work of the world's wage earners. Moreover, with the growth of a new amount of human creative work that is stimulated and dictated by capital in a controlled manner, the degree of independent creative and self-creative quantity and quality of human creative work grows, which constantly and intensively breaks through the layer of legal control and dictates of private capital. Just as human creative and self-creative work created the legal dictate of capital as the means by which mankind has made the greatest progress over the past millennia, it is to be expected that the growth of the quantity and quality of human wage labor over time will completely eliminate the dictate of private capital as a feature which possessively limits and controls creativity in favor of private property and create new conditions and means for creative and self-creative work that generates new values without the dictates and legality of private capital.

QUESTIONS THAT ARISE

If we go back to the relations of modern practice presented by the trinity of wage earners (live current work) wage earners of capital owners (owners of past objectified labor) and the very property of capital dictate (the sum of all capital values that imperatively obliges communities to create more than the current total) which dictates every creative and self-creative relation, the question arises as to who is the protagonist or rational living creative subject in this trinity that significantly affects each subsequent step of progress, if we keep in mind that, after the accumulation and formation of new potential operating capital reproduction given by the magnitude of the initial values of capital and the imperative dictate of capital as a general and operational value that becomes a general planned social value cared for by all governments of the world by their unlimited legality and operational functions. All the more so as this general rational dictatorship of capital is elaborated in every and the smallest form of instructions and given conditions defined in the legal system that fully define us and, if necessary, of that same capital and its rational dictatorship, those acts or dictates are legally added to the "democratic procedures" with new rules if the old ones are tight or unusable for the existing, new and efficient survival and growth of capital. It is certainly quite difficult to judge objectively whether the development of democracies so far throughout world history has promoted submissive service to capital or whether democracy has consciously agreed to serve the dictatorship of capital and capital relations because there are no other tools. Almost all the revolutionary changes that our world history remembers and knows, even though they were initiated by some form of capital dictatorship, although in their resolutions they have written maxims pointing to the abolition of some experiential form of capital relations are being completed again and a new cycle of their new revolutionary practice with a new capital relation that will over time become the cause of a new revolution. Precisely for this reason, it is inevitable for the existing modern practice of capital and capital relations that its quantitative and qualitative characteristics will continue to grow and develop as part of total creative resources or as part of human creative both past material work and live current work. It is equally inevitable to state that the subject of creation is not only wage earners who own capital together with the legal system and forms of government which is constantly changing by adapting the mass (as large) creative subject of creative human work of wage earners to its functional survival, but also the overall calculation of operational functions of the whole society that we marked as a layer of the imperative dictate of capital, they are only a part of the capital subordinated to the functional stratification of modern productive communities.

Regarding this, another essential question arises for the definition of the subject of creation and self-creation in human history and society: do all three subjects in symbiosis break through the layer of the dictatorship of capital and when? Or, in the "deviation" towards new values, they are recognizable in these features that break through the layer of capital dictatorship veil as exclusively creative and self-creative properties of wage labor (in our terminology we would like the reader to see wage earner has a far wider scope and meaning than typical stereotypes slave, serf or proletarian class in classical sociological analysis) which creates a new value from which accumulation and new capital are formed. When we say exclusively then we really mean that in the symbiosis of this creative trinity of wage earners, capitalists as owners or managers with capital and whole capital we recognize that capitalists as fully owners of capital or its managers work creatively and self-creatively with values previously realized in past wage labor that becomes a static value of the most varied forms and potentials. One of the most important predispositions of past work is its constant openness to both quantitative and quality supplementation of its potential and predispositions. The past materialized work of all wage earners is a fundamental means of directing the new current creative and self-creative work of wage earners, which in new cycles creates a completely new value dictated by the rational immanent culture of memory of all capital...

WHO ARE WAGE EARNERS?

By studying and observing the natural evolutionary processes of all living beings, scientists have come to the conclusion that in every microcosm of evolutionary development, but also in nature as a whole, there are fundamental and responsible carriers of all functional coexistence and flora and fauna which would usually be called "key stone" (in architecture it is the central stone in the arch) or the principal foundation stone on which the entire building or structure is based. And in the case of living beings, the whole life and overall survival of biological communities in both the micro and macro spheres. Of course, during his evolutionary and later revolutionary historical creative and self-creative development, the human being grew into the absolutely most influential form of the "keystone" of modern historical and evolutionary but also revolutionary creative reality characterized by his fully conscious creative and self-creative activity. The development of human active creative and self-creative activity and in connection with that the formation of his consciousness significantly affects and reaches the most distant spheres not only of the flora and fauna of this planet but also the essential properties of all chemical elements of which this planet is made. Through his creative and self-creative work, the human being, during his creative and self-creative development, imposed himself as a fundamental property of the surface-active harmony of the Planet Earth. Although the negative consequences of human influence on nature and society are constantly visible, its influence still dominates. The basic means with which the human being, during his especially conscious and self-creative development, used to become a fundamental and principled determinant is the dictate of capital and the capital relations. Using this tool, the human creative being has formed all the bad and all the good values, but also a whole series of still completely unknown interventions in the process, both in nature and in the social environments in which we live as social beings. Objective quantitative and qualitative balances and analyzes of our evolutionary and creative self-creative activities that are comprehensive for the entire Planet Earth and the part of the universe we gravitate to do not exist.

What we use legally and what exists are singular or par-ticular analyzes of scientists selected by capital and capital relations by giving legal priority only to those reviews that are the basis of the pragmatic increase of dominant capital.

Let us return to the description of the basic features of wage creative work which is the "key stone" of the entire human creative and self-creative history without which no part of our modern or future civilization could survive. We will use a spiral presentation of the growth and develop-ment of materialized human labor, live current labor and the basic features of breaking through the dictatorship of capital with the primary task of determining who is the subject of this breakthrough of the dictatorship of capi-tal not only today but during our historical development. We have already emphasized in the text that not a cent of new capital in any society would be created or record-ed in the GDP of modern countries if wage earners did not go to work every day and if the health of these wage earners was not usable. Likewise, without the presence of human ongoing creative and self-creative work, past ma-terialized labor turned into the means of production would simply be neglected and its potential functions would dis-appear. Factories of all kinds of organization in the field of material production, domestic corporations, interna-tional corporations, power plants, transport, agriculture, maritime, organization, life of urban communities and megalopolises, rural areas, schools, universities, hospital libraries, shops, manufacturers and information technol-ogy functions and technologies, science and scientific research, journalism, cultural institutions and art of all kinds would rapidly die out without their materialized past work and memory present in current creative and self-creative live work.

In the earlier historical development of man and society and in the flow of existing reality, the appearance of wage earners is defined by specific properties of the value of past work which, as part of his current work of earlier creative and self-creative experience, the individual adopted and integrated as a memory from himself and about himself in his own psychophysical active being and his recognizable social function. With these predispositions defined by the universal law of motion and its active creative and self-creative rational being, each individual has a natural and social right to participate in work and creativity in societies where he works, grows up, reproduces, creates and dies. In the characteristics of his own being, each wage earner has integrated all predispositions of possession and management not only with his past work which is immanent and contained in his physical personality but also with objects which he achieved in the same process of creative and self-creative work that are part of the use values that other wage earners recognize in specific social relations. Just as the use values of natural objects are estimated, we also estimate the use values of our own work, but also the use values of another human being and ourselves.

The difference between the value and quantity materialized from the past work of the wage earner who creates the use object and the past work of the wage earner who forms the creative and self-creative personality in the same procedure is that the created use objects lose their permanent material properties, unlike wage earner self-creation, which in the same process of constant creation generates a permanently greater memory of the INDEPENDENT human creative psyche that re-forms a new object and itself as a new creative and self-creative quantity and quality. We recognize the individualism of the wage personality as well as the overall social values in the use and possession of active memory values of previous past work that we use in the process of creation in live current work... The use values that our creative and self-creative being consciously creates are our primary social attributes with which we begin to socially present our creative personality to other human beings incredibly early (essentially immediately after birth).

LAYERS OF WAGE EARNERS

As much as in reproductive cycles we prefer human wage labor to the creation of use values primarily of material production but also the value of every other production, the creative and self-creative human being never consumes or realizes in its existential processes the complete consumption of these products. Most of the production value is intended for the market and the consumption of the values created by the society in which the creators operate, regardless of how they were organized. This consumption is controlled and dosed by the dictates of capital as well as by the dictates of every known capital relation in the history so far, which primarily prefers control of production and consumption of use values of past and live current wage creative and self-creative work. In other words, organized control of creative and self-creative work and life flows of wage earners consumption of all strata that lasts and forms an endless active memory of current work that we socialize without borders becomes the only guarantee of survival of capital dictates and capital relations. Creative and self-creative memory, which is recognized both in its reach and as extremely creative knowledge but also as ignorance in the possession of almost all layers of wage earners is just such a guarantee of creation and survival of all new and quantitatively and qualitatively valuable reproductive cycles that enrich and create new accumulation and new capital. The symbiosis of the dictates of capital and the current labor of wage earners and their creative and self-creative values or capital in the form of human creative current labor is much stronger than the symbiosis of capital with static objects or past material labor that do not possess independent creative production of new use values. In other words, to possess and dispose of human current creative and self-creative work is much more important than to possess the riches of the widest spectrum without the possibility of disposing of human current work.

The capital belonging to the capitalist arose from earlier past wage labor and he uses it according to his needs through the market and known market criteria and legal capital relations for the employment of wage earners by the hour, day, month, a year, two years... or indefinitely. We see the layers of wage earners best in tax elaborations where we also recognize their primary qualitative-qualitative labels and the predispositions of the primary consumption of their wages in wage earners families and primary groups in the communities where they live. Their income is also an indication of their current usable potential market wage or stand-alone hybrid entrepreneurial wage value that changes and which, through these changes in production and consumption cycles, informs the rest of the reproductive community about their new usable pragmatic value in a particular current work process belonging to new circumstances and a concrete new dictate of capital.

If we go back to the basic determinants of the legal law described in our maxim, emphasizing that part of the text which stresses that all values created by the work of wage earners in modern corporations and all other types of capital relations, belong to the owner of the capital or employer, we must know that every wage earner in the process of his creative and self-creative work generates the expected or greater amount of value than the value of wages itself. Otherwise, if he does not achieve this higher value, he loses his status of pragmatic variable capital or active creative and self-creative being. The implementation of this legal maxim that we explain earlier that is legally used by modern capital and the capital relation essentially conditions the wage earner to be a creative and self-creative being, but does not proclaim him in the legislation of his legal systems as a fundamental creator of new social values with the right to enter into the division of newly created value recorded in social relations after the payment of wages and outside the known wage price, which does not change often and persistently for decades or often shows a tendency to fall. The first thing we must note is that in current reproductive processes there is not a single element that defines the actual wage use value contained and recorded in the created use value of the finished object of his current work. That object and its use value belong to the owner of capital who dictates the market values of wage earners as well as the whole cycle of social reproduction which is under the control of capital and capital relations and previous transferred past labor and new current labor of wage earners to the extent dictated by capital and its owner. The owner of the capital who pays for the current work of the wage earner, in addition to the amount of capital with which he pays for the wage earner labor, also has a memory of the past work of the wage earner (universal society memory) which he does not often pay on the market. From the entire memory of past work that is available to everyone, capital and its owner primarily prefer the use of dynamic creative and self-creative (universal movement) features of live current work, because, according to all instructions of the total memory of historical human creativity, they know that this live creative human work generates new and quantitative and qualitative values that are transformed by legal systems created for this purpose into its new accumulation, capital and profit.

This wage compensation and its value defined on the labor market belonging to the wage earner as compensation for his current work in the calculations of capitalists and owners of capital before the current labor process is regularly defined in the minds of capital owners as a source of future capital accumulation, but also as a sum that, in minimal amounts, elements the daily life of wage earners and society as a whole. The market wage compensation can in no way be compared and marked as the equivalent of the real value of the current wage labor at their disposal and which is entirely appropriated by the capitalist. This is the main reason why the legal maxim that is the means of dictatorship of capital and capital relations is defined so that all newly created values of current work are attributed to the owner of capital. Such an important and essential maxim as legal law of the dictates of capital will exist as long as there are social systems that nurture capital and the capital relation as a means of creating accumulation, capital, and profit for private or social owners of capital. While this maxim exists, it will always be emphasized in legal systems that all values of wage labor that the owner or user of capital realizes through the work of wage earners hired and paid on the labor market with their capital (VK variable capital) belong primarily only to the private owner of capital or bureaucratic systems of capital users in a capital relation. The owner of the capital always has the total newly created value created in the creative and self-creative work of the wage earner, which belongs to him after the wage has been paid. With this status and legally protected feature, he is regularly given the goal to define the pragmatics of new reproductive cycles and the accumulation of new capital in his favor. When, on the other hand, and on the contrary to the newly created new reproductive values, accumulation and new capital in the sphere of production of means of production and production of means of consumption in social relations, we see the innumerable layered social structure of those who also need those newly created values since they cannot survive without them, we must ask ourselves who and in what way elements and enables the work of these layers of wage earners or consumers of new value who are not wage earners - direct producers in the sphere of material production where primary newly created values arise. Of course, the answer to this question is always addressed to the owners of accumulation and capital within social reproduction who dictate pragmatic consumption of newly created value under special conditions of capital consumption, thus enabling the survival and functions of the wider social community. Consumers of this consumption, as well as wage earners in the field of material consumption, are regularly defined as a pragmatic part of the circulation of accumulation, capital and profit, otherwise the owners of newly created capital in the sphere of material production cannot use it. Every wage earner is capital itself, a value he wants to maintain on a scale of values and comparison with other layers of capital in reproductive cycles, yet we see that most world wage earners have a recognizably modest amount of value with which they cannot significantly influence the capitalist and change the procedure for valuing the current work of wage earners from previously realized capital on the labor market. In such arranged societies and reproductive cycles controlled by the owner of dominant sums, a capital that always increases the amount and power of dominant capital at the expense of the wage earner and self-creators, the role of wage earner is primarily characterized by its constant maintenance at the minimum of functional standard and earnings, which cannot substantially change its formal and legal status in existing democratic communities. Changes do not require legal democracy, nor a legal moral code of maxims that favors dominant capital, the accumulation and formation of capital created by the work of wage earners in the possession of private or social bureaucratic capital, but a scientific and moral general principle code and legal system that will choose the generally accepted key definition of the real subject, the creator and the process of creation of newly created value. In order to achieve this, the basic condition is the elimination of the very maxim that we interpret in the text which is the broadest basis of the mirage on which the modern capitalist system grew, which places the owner of capital or manager with accumulation and capital in the role of legal primary creator in live current work. How to achieve a new socio-economic system without this maxim with rational creative goals and moral ethical principles without legality and legal morality as we know it today is not defined in today's history and its modern trends. The only support of modern humanity is the indomitable fundamental predispositions of the creative and self-creative work of the wage earners of the world, which function in all historical circumstances. They have yet to be given a new universal meaning.

CAPITALIST AS A WAGE EARNER

The capitalist system of the creation and accumulation of capital does not exclude anyone, nor is it possible from a subordinate position to capital itself in all known capital relations in the processes of production of newly created value. The typical status characteristics of the owner of capital, although the maxim with which he subordinates the lower classes of wage earners in the market works in his favor, which we encounter in modern social life in which they are present as a subject of social reproduction, are reduced to wage or maintenance and increase of existing equity the reproductive processes of his corporation or any other investment creation with which he participates in the overall reproductive relations of the whole society. In these operations, which he directs together or without advisors and managers, the operational determinant and goal of each reproduction cycle is to increase accumulation, capital and profit through market wage earners but also their own wage work for which they also receive compensation or personal income. If the increase of accumulation, capital of profit is not realized in reproductive processes in known legal political and economic systems in which it participates, his engaged daily wage action subordinated to the tasks imposed on him by his own capital, the wage earning capital owner remains without compensation or accumulation of capital, which is reflected and transferred to the absence of compensation to other wage earners in all social strata, primarily wage earnings in the primary reproductive cycle. To prevent economic cataclysms from occurring with tragic consequences, the owners of accumulation and capital have created their own dictates of social reproduction and their legal right to manage the wage values of past work and live current work based on the described maxim and its everyday pragmatic applications which oblige and define all wage participants in the reproductive process as a social creative and self-creative being subject to modern capital. Pursuant to the legal right to dispose of variable capital based on that maxim, that is, wage labor, it is the right of every owner of capital to determine the market price of wage labor. The range of wage benefits from minimum to maximum always gravitates to the minimum wage guaranteed by law. In this way, the owner of capital ensures a safe and known price of wage labor that is stable and at the same time creates a distance from the rights of wage earners to participate in the distribution of accumulation, capital and profits in the use and turnover value of objects to be realized in social capital relation. The greater the private capital in the possession of the wage-earner capitalist, the greater the affection and protection of his creative and self-creative reproductive activities and functions by the legal, political, and economic system in modern capitalist and socialist society around the world. This protection and tolerant relationship of the legal, political, and economic system also applies to the capitalist himself, whether he is the individual or group owner of capital or the corporation with which he participates in reproductive cycles. ("Too big to fail" is a rational general principle of capital protection of all communities in which the capital relation is the dominant social relation)

The comfortable life of wealthy capitalists often creates the illusion of complete independence from the dictates of capital and capital relations, which is not true. The right to decisions on the primary division of the value of wage labor of wage earners paid in the labor market based on the maxim created by the owner of private capital and incorporated into the legal, political and economic system to use capital as a means of dictate is the source of his private property as well as personal wage earnings in the corporation of which he is the owner or co-owner. Likewise, the maxim is the foundation of the newly formed accumulation and capital of a corporation that is partially or wholly owned by him. With this realized private capital and the capital of the company of which he is a partial or majority owner, he has the primary possibility of hiring not only market wage earners in primary production but also wage earners who are quality managers and executives who know well the content of the process of creating and maintaining capital and all the pragmatic achievements and benefits of doing business and participating in the political, legal and economic system of the society in which they participate. Of particular importance is the relationship between the financial capital of the wider community (state-owned banks) and ownership of own and corporate capital, which is based on the protectorate principle "the greater the capital, the greater its protection and the possibility of increasing it." The owner does not have to participate in the management of the company, but his work, which is in a wage-wage rental relationship with his own capital, also defines the remuneration for work.

His participation in the company's business is regularly rewarded: a) with a salary, b) a bonus or reward at the end of the year, c) percentage share in the profit, d) a reward for advisory function and specific assistance in doing business and other forms of reward.

Although the formal status of the wage earner and the wage earning owner is the same, the wage earner who owns capital differs significantly in reality from the usual wage earner in that he is given the legal opportunity to use the right to appropriate the newly created value (profit and accumulation) of his wage earners, which is what the maxim refers to, realized in the statements b), c), d), to which the ordinary wage earner is usually not entitled. Second, the wage-earning owner of capital is given the opportunity to directly manage the accumulation, capital and profit generated by the work of market wage earners who are denied this opportunity. There are also many other benefits such as for example covering all the costs of the owner, both private and company, which he realizes as well as many other benefits. Small business owners up to 3,000,000 dollars, are really no different from ordinary non-owner wage earners whose annual earnings are $ 65,000 - $ 180,000. The reason for this is in the very narrow accumulation and new capital. Yet in the world's most developed economy, such as the US economy, owner's wages and recorded incomes reach fabulous, almost incomprehensible heights. We see this in the incomes of Amazon owner Jeff Bezos. Here are these analytical figures and sketches to compare with the rest of the wage earners both in the USA and the world. Jeff Bezos' monthly income, 6.54 billion, b) 1-1 / 5 billion per week, c) 215 million per day, d) 8-9 million per hour, e) 140,000 dollars per minute. We must certainly not forget that Jeff Bezos' losses are just as big if they occur in the volatile market for the services and use values that Amazon offers. Similar to the ownership status is the position of general managers (CEOs) and managers, with amounts of income illustrating their wages from the minimum we have already mentioned to multimillion sums and other bonuses that belong to them. In medium-sized companies over 500 employees and large companies that they often employ 10,000,20,000 and significantly more workers the range of salaries of directors and managers range from $ 17,000,000 to $ 80,000,000 dollars per year, probably even significantly more in larger companies. Every penny that ends up in their private earnings other than what we call wages or personal earnings deserved by their creative work, is created by the synchronized work of the entire wage body of the corporation they manage and the differences shown here in the wage price when comparing the minimum and maximum wage gains rising up to 100 times higher than the average wage earnings are possible only because of its foundation in the maxim that the profit from materialized past labor and live current labor of all wage earners employed in corporations belongs essentially to the capital of the corporation, its owners and management. They are also creators of these rules of accumulation and distribution of the newly created value of all wage earners who participate in the reproductive process, which go back to the deep history of past work. We will try to illustrate what this means to have such a legal status as the owners and management of companies, by presenting the results of capital accumulation of companies resulting from the reduction of tax liabilities of American corporations initiated by the administration of current President D. Trump from 35% to 21% accepted by the American democratic parliamentary system without significant criticism or amendment in USA Congress or Senate. Such decision was made as a typical example of obtaining enormous benefits for the capital and wage earners of the owners of American dominant capital, but not for the benefit of the entire social system and the population of American wage earners. The layered presentation of the impact of this decision and the recognition of benefits for the entire wage population in the USA shows a significant increase in employment of all layers of wage earners, but not the growth of wage earners compensation, which has been stagnant for 60 years. Benefits for lower-paid wage earners are mainly related to the possibility of additional work outside the standard of 8 hours of work. The increase in the number of hours worked by American wage earners certainly indicates the possibility of earning, unfortunately, within the value of wages or hours of work that is unchanged for 60 years for the American wage earner. This increased quantum of labor for corporations, on the other hand, points to a remarkable new profit illustrated by a greater amount of wage labor and, as we have pointed out, lower corporate taxes. The experience of two years of implementation of the reduction of corporate tax liabilities is not fully felt among low-income wage earners. It is important to understand that democratic political decisions that define laws and changes in the law, for all in the American Parliament, are most often based on tendencies of apologetic science and general socialization in favor of capital and capital relations and defense of dominant capital tendencies in the existing conservative and traditional state of consciousness, which are regularly most represented in the pragmatic system and visions of the US Congress and Senate. Making "vital decisions" in favor of capital and traditional capital relations also indicates a great lack of new balanced, pragmatic solutions that apply to society as a whole and the community. This is considered by congressional and senate delegates if they are in the over-half majority representing republican interests or the extreme right, as in other parliaments of world communities where the capital and capital relations dominate. In this process of making decisions on new laws or their repeal, there is a lack of objective indicators and the practice of implementing these political decisions that we see in all wage-earning classes, which is a big problem. This is also noticeable in the decision to reduce the tax liabilities of American corporations by 14%. When a 14% reduction in taxes places American entrepreneurs in the world's dominant trillion-dollar business ($ 21 trillion GDP in 2019 in the USA), it is noticeable that the new free capital that appears has countless investment and creative potentials, especially in the form of financial capital and borrowing in order to expand business both within the USA and outside the USA, everywhere in the world where the possibility of making a profit is indicated. Unfortunately, this decision to reduce

US corporate tax liabilities does not mention direct legal benefits to wage earners and self-creators of US corporate profits, accumulation and capital, which would be a logical consequence of the resulting tax reduction benefits, all the more so because all future workflows and reproduction functions are done by these same US wage earners to maintain corporate accumulation of capital and profits in the new US reproduction cycles. Unfortunately, the wage earner is a respected business partner of a capitalist society only up to a conditional market agreement that dictates the price of his work. This is where his significant influence on corporate business ends. His further characteristics within the capital relations of the whole society in which he operates and creates are marked by the power of his wage earnings and the tax rules imposed on him in the reproductive cycle by the dominant capital for which he works in corporations as a wage earner.

In the new tax brackets that have been in force for three years, which bind the American citizen, almost nothing has fundamentally changed. Especially in these tax liabilities, there are no radical percentage reductions in the taxation of the American wage-earning population that would match or be similar to the 14% reduction in the taxes of corporate business. Nowhere is there an increase in the income of wage earners and their wages, which is defined by a direct percentage increase in market wages, which would be a logical consequence of new possible investments in the quality and quantity of variable capital that appears after the reduction of corporate tax liabilities. For wage earning capital owners who are reluctant to agree to any increase in wage benefits, which we see in this case, is far more profitable traditional practice indicated by modern practice in the USA that maximizes the quantitative actual and potential value of wage labor based on unincreased (dictated) wages or investments in the work of domestic or wage earners around the world, which are still far cheaper than US wage earners and with which the placement of dominant capital is far simpler due to the needs of open investment programs of all kinds. A private owner of capital has no legal reciprocal obligation to divide the capital created, whether created by the work of a wage earner or by a political decision of a legislature, which the legal system allows him to register in his private account or in his corporation's account after the wages paid to their wage earners and the payment of other social obligations and expenses. Such obligations of private owners of capital and corporations are nowhere recorded either in the basic law of all citizens of the USA (Constitution) or in other laws. But the future of the symbiosis of the creator and self-creator of the newly created value or the wage-earner of the world and capital will be arranged in a different way. One day when capital owners realize that the increase in the quality and quantity of wage creative and self-creative current labor is much faster in the growth of their total values than the growth of accumulation and private dominant capital that cannot control it, the institutions created by capital will disappear. The accumulation of creative and self-creative values that is already happening in favor of wage earners is not just a political proclamation but a daily growth in the quality and quantity of creative and self-creative current and past work of wage earners with a broad demographic basis that also increases with the initial stage of geometric progression. To what extent absolute control of the accumulation and creation of capital in future reproductive processes is possible in the traditional dictated capitalist way in the whole world is not entirely clear to anyone. The presence of the demographic factor, but primarily the growth of qualitative and quantitative characteristics of world wage earners created in their creative work is a more pronounced fundamental corrector of the process of both production and consumption that essentially defines accumulation, capital and profit.

Increasing the quality of life and social standards in which wage earners reside is an important and lacking condition that significantly affects their efficiency in creative and self-creative work within reproductive cycles as was the case in American society in the 1950s and 1960s after World War II when both the private and social standard of wage earners was considerably higher than it is today, when the orientation to the growth of capital and its dictate grew to the level of the exclusive goal of its owners.

Unfortunately, the modern political, legal, and economically oriented USA nowhere lists the benefits that would arise for wage earners from reducing taxes for corporations as a legal determinant. It can be noticed that, for example, the growth of bank profits was extremely high in 2018, 2019 at all banks as a direct consequence of the increase and circulation of new capital, but no citizen as a saver or obligor and payer of credit obligations for a loan to buy a house received any notice of percentage equivalent participation and benefits in these accumulative automatisms of bank capital in which each wage earner is a participant both as their original creator and as a saver or possibly a small investor. To illustrate what is essentially happening: if you have $ 100,000 in a bank for a year, your money is managed by the bank administration and at the end of that one-year period each "saver" gets his bank interest earnings as provided on the day of investment. The bank turns over your money as part of its capital on the money market so that its interest (financial capital) is paid at a rate of 15% -25%. It would be logical for each saver to receive an interest amount appropriate to that bank's interest earnings. But this is not what is happening. American citizens with small savings are forced to operate their daily functional needs through banks on their savings in today's conditions cannot get more than 0% -1% interest savings, and 3% to 5% for 5 year fixed-term deposits. If you want higher earnings for your money in a bank account, you are forced to enter your money in the stock market, independently or with the assistance of a bank broker of the same bank where your savings are or some other bank or institution. Other types of investments are possible with the assistance of bank loans if you manage to prove your creditworthiness with your capital. The problem is not the investment scheme and the opportunities that are offered to you, but the investment uncertainty and serious lack of information about the essential flows of the shareholder business of the average citizen.

It seems that Trump's decisions to reduce taxes from 35% to 21% of revenues are really intended to strengthen the position of only that part of capital that essentially determines the dominant dictatorship of the traditional capital relation. Employment growth and the availability of new jobs that are a direct consequence of the expansion of the corporate business resulting in a 14% reduction in taxes is also the basic benefit of all wage earners, especially those in lower tax brackets offered by owners of dominant capital. It is almost impossible to comprehend the hypocrisy of this legislative decision that favors the dominant large capital of private owners and corporations and the existing capital relations, while neglecting the real and formal creators of American wages earners and citizens who are part of that capital and its essential dictated and conditioned creators (variable capital) without which capital would not exist at all. The US $ 21 trillion GDP held by private owners and corporations is 14% tax-free, and it is not entirely known what is happening with these new values and money. Part of that money will certainly be spent on increasing wage labor, as already shown by the experiences and statistics on the employment of American citizens in the two-year implementation of this tax law so far.

With the new increase in wage labor population in the USA, the legal forms of laws passed by the US Congress and Senate that indicate wage gains and the formation of new profits and capital intended for the wage population, which the wage labor market would have to count on in a new way, are not publicly visible. The one-sided preference of American political and legislative bodies for capital owners is evident in the case of the reduction of corporate tax liabilities in the modern flow of American practice and American capital relations, as many times before. This practice still does not indicate the creative and self-creative importance of the market wage population in all wage functions, which is the only majority of the social class that permanently increases the quantity and quality of the existing capital, which the complete present and future of social communities depend on.

Attachments: 7, and 8. Shift and increase of the existing capital veil layer.

We have already graphically illustrated in Attachment: 7 the ever-increasing and spiraling growth of the interaction of past (red) and live current work (green) of wage earners and self-creators creating all the new use values needed by the human being and human communities. This creative wage labor generates a new accumulation of capital, but also all changes and new forms of capital relations, which over time are best illustrated by the total amount of capital invested in the material past labor of the means of production and in the live work of wage earners and their productive communities. Engaged capital, which is constantly growing and conditioning new work and new accumulation, capital and profit is referred to as the veil layer of capital that is constantly growing and is marked in purple in this book and in our graphics.

A series of smaller spirals of dark green color whose arrows pierce and move the veil layer of capital (purple) to a larger volume (drawn purple) represents the current wage labor of all wage earners in reproductive relations without which this growth of accumulation, capital and profit that would form a new veil layer of potential capital (accumulation, profit and new capital) would be completely unattainable.

The red arrow indicates the direction of continuous vortex spiral growth and development of all reproductive and creative processes in human communities that we recognize in materialized past work and live current work. In later text, we will provide a quantified and qualified overview of their importance for increasing total accumulation and total US capital by presenting the tax brackets in which American wage earners are placed in accordance with their earnings.

CAPITAL AS A DEITY

Wage earning for one's own capital is a daily creative

obligation of private owners of both small and large capital. The wages of people, creators and self-creators in current work who have no other characteristics than their market value are always recorded as potential capital in their possession, and in traditional political economy we have placed wage peculiarities in variable capital which capitalists, together with means of production or materialized past and wage earners current work, realize in the reproductive processes of production of means of production and production of means of consumption. Our approach to understanding wage earners has a broader scope in which, in relation to the dictates of capital in existing capital, the relations of social communities and the capital owner and wage earner who is not in possession of capital are in an identical relationship. The stratification of wage earners and analysis of their social status indicate that general subordination to the dictates of capital limits and controls the income with which market wage earners are formed. What limits them and keeps them at the level of market wages are legal systems, appropriated and created by the wage earners - owners of dominant capital, that are used as a means of maintaining private accumulation and capital by the same owners of dominant capital.

In addition to the legal acquisition of capital from wage labor, wage earners who own dominant capital (01% wage earners population) also acquire the right to organize the socio-political and economic reproduction of their communities.

Unlike traditional wage earners, owners of large sums of capital begin their wage earning activity in planning the legal process of converting the value of wage labor they pay in the labor market with their capital in the form of wages into new accumulation and capital in their favor. This process can last throughout the life of the capitalist, but the process can disappear with the emergence of conditions during his life and work that lead to the loss of total capital and cessation of reproductive work of wage earners within the wage framework of variable capital of a corporation or company owned by the capitalist. It is not possible to present the total wage functions of the owners of capital without mentioning and describing the divine position of the transcendent and potential sums of capital that we plan and create in our consciousness through wage labor. There is not a single human being, no matter what socio-political system he lives in, who does not constantly identify with the power of capital. Both the capitalist citizen and the socialist citizen, as well as the creators of earlier human history, are marked by the subjective will to possess and power which they recognize in the geometric progression of capital increase created by human wage labor and its legal subordination to capital and capital relations. We always strive for new and larger sums in all the capital creation processes that are available. Those realized sums that we spend on materialized past work and live current work and replenish from the value of realized wage labor into new larger sums than the initial starting sums of capital intended for a certain production and creative and self-creative process recorded by the legal system also allow omnipotent legal distance between wage earners - creators of accumulation and capital on the one hand and the legal possibility of recording the geometric growth of the value of part of someone else's work in their ownership and jurisdiction, based on the capital invested in reproductive processes. The greater the amount of invested capital, the greater the sum of its geometric records in the sum of total accumulation and capital for its investor. This rule is regularly realized in an economic reality that has a stable upward trajectory of capital accumulation. The period of economic stagnation or cataclysm regularly gives priority to that layer of wage earners who in the earlier period registered in their favor a significant amount of accumulation and capital. This is primarily because these wage earners and owners of capital are again the basic legal initiators of new reproductive cycles in which wage earners without accumulated capital in earlier creative periods are re-employed through a controlled market. The value of accumulation and capital is regularly recorded in the private ownership of each wage earner. During the process of creative work in the previous current past work of all wage earners during human history, and from modern permanent creative functions of current work of market wage earners and wage earners of capital owners within the new creative reproduction, an independent sum of divine omnipotent capital is formed, multiplied by creative and self-creative current work of all wage earners. Its whirling spiral quantified and qualified deity (value) is the untouchable private property of the capitalist wage earners with which they govern social communities. This private possession of the increased sum of accumulation and capital is legally protected by legal systems that protect the legal rights of possession of capital based on the values of wage labor of market wage earners. Capital possesses endless alternatives of survival (power) in modern social relations in which it primarily defines, through the legal economic and political system, transcendent independent divine power over the wage-earning population without the possession of capital, which it constantly entrusts to increase accumulation and capital. It is equally important to note that the omnipotent properties of capital accumulation appropriate to the times in which we live as well as that its divine power and independence disappear from the historical scene if its wage earners disappear.

Imagine owning a corporation worth a total of $ 1 trillion belongs to you in whole or in part and that you manage together with your managers in the creative processes of producing new utility items that the world market is interested in. Imagine that your starting position is a static sum of 1 trillion dollars that must not be kept in that position because otherwise you become a loser. This dictated imaginary threat that comes to the fore in our consciousness as the owner of that capital is at the same time the horizon that looms over the transcendent commanding deity (capital) to which you aspire as its functional wage-maker. A creative dream based on our own capital which we realize in the well-established legal patterns of capital relations of different profiles of capitalism and socialism throughout history, with which we reach the increased omnipotent transcendence of capital in our consciousness and in our human being which has socialized capital forms in fact does not know our complete creative identity unless our wage-earning personality identifies with the supernatural power of capital in everyday practice. This magnetic power of capital constantly drives us into omnipotent unattainable illusions dictated only by mythical divine beings, offering us unattainable expanses of paradise or punishment.

These are also the primary characteristics of every human being or his capital-marked visible value in practice, be it the small ones related to the poorest wage earners or to the richest wage earners we meet every day in our social life. This wage-earning dream of the deity of capital essentially and ruthlessly marks the owner of the dominant capital who participates in all the pragmatic functions of the creation of newly created accumulation and capital. Unlike the lower classes of wage earners who do not own large sums of capital or material human labor but only wages from current labor, his wages are tied not only to the 8-hour or 16-hour wage but also to permanent work and capital creation as well as the social relationship of capitalism or socialism that allows this without temporal, spatial or any other limitation. The social relationship of building sustainability and direct participation in communities that are a cohesion legal framework that allows for the legality of dominant capital and capital relation is essentially inaccessible to wage earners who own smaller amounts of capital in the existing legal parliamentary system. The fundamental reason why this is so lies in the necessary operative transmission of the basic features of the dictates of capital constantly present in our primary creative consciousness of every wage earner to create, increase and register larger sums of capital in his favor with minimal political participation. The dictates of capital regularly by their very nature and almost automatically, as indicated by earlier historical practice, form legal protection and preference for larger sums and accumulations of capital that indicate independent prosperity.

The greater the capital in possession... it also becomes a principled moral earthly means and the source of every apologetics of the dictates of capital, owners and managers of capital, which by a series of legal instruments conditions the dictated reproductive position of market wage earners who do not own capital to ensure pragmatic programs of realization of dominant capital belonging to a small number of wage earners and its registration in and through the legal, political and economic system in a complex dictate of capital as a general culture of existence. Another reason can be found in the conditioned insufficient creation and possession of investment capital among market wage earners, especially lower incomes, which is a necessary means of reasonable domination in the social participation of capitalist and socialist social communities today in their reproductive cycles. Regardless of whether the investor-wage earner buys and enters his own completely private company or participates through the stock market, which is the most accessible form of participation in the division of newly formed accumulation, capital and profit of the companies that are already available on the stock market, the starting and expected result are always better with larger amounts of equity provided they enter a healthy and proven business environment. Even on the stock exchanges, lower-wage earners do not generate significant income due to the minimal investments that are possible for their income. The third and probably the most important condition in the daily life of wage earners around the world, which conditions them to be obedient servants of the dictates of capital, lies in the completely disparate cohesion of common interests of wage earners within their stratification which is essentially extremely important and powerful and can be a crucial support for the progress of the whole society. This common support of all wage earners of the world to recognize themselves as a social force (key stone) and the foundation of the progress of social reproductions in modern creative and self-creative cultures is missing and can be said to be a fundamental missing link in general efforts to progress.

This is especially evident in the election procedures of social communities for the identification and election of officials and delegates to the functions of local, state, or federal administrative representative and executive authorities. Election to these representative positions cannot be obtained only with a good program offered by delegates, but this is achieved with investment money that frequently promotes the delegate and his program through aggressive information and political marketing throughout the election process. Most often, this politically informative marketing is a sweet-talking compilation of visions offered in conjunction with dominant capital. Those enormous sums of capital that are spent in election procedures belong to those investors to whom political parties are eternal debtors. On the other hand, even the minimum amounts of money allocated to these election programs are completely inaccessible to most wage earners in the world, and most often their impact on the political, legal and economic system is reduced to voting functions, often apathetic motivation (static impotence) in which not even half of citizens participate. Voting obligation is a remarkable potential for the future wage earners stratification of capitalism and socialism provided that wage earners define their social interests and characteristics as dominant capital parallel to any dominant capital that governs in a way the capital relations manage social reproductions. Motivation to vote in the future for wage earners if they want to change their social position will also be marked by organized investment programs that will be implemented smoothly after the election process because they will also be majority programs. The programs offered by the current political parties in power characterize the position of wage earners exclusively as a tool and means of capital and not as a creative subject of reproductive processes. Basically, without such programs that will define a strong cohesive force of wage earners interests, neither the democratic election procedures themselves, nor the post-election democratic function, nor the creative and self-creation work of wage earners will significantly deviate from the existing forms of capital relations.

RECORDING OF PRIVATE CAPITAL.... OR CAPITAL RELATIONS

The statistics of the IRS (Internal Revenue Service) of the joint American service, which records the total income and tax of taxpayers on personal income and personal capital created in the USA for each current year, recorded the simultaneous payment of taxes of all American wage earners, citizens and institutions (corporations) which had achieved a new one-year GDP and their own income. In this way, by separating taxes from their income, wage earners and citizens participate in creating both their own and the net income of the American Federation, which is recorded after mandatory tax calculations in the IRS. Wage earners income is currently generated by 141,200,000 million tax-paying wage earners we recognize in GDP, in which we have placed the entire stratification and work of wage earners and citizens of all kinds, amounts to 18.620 trillion dollars for 2016. We call this amount the Gros Domestic Product or GDP for 2016. GDP is formed and recorded in the sum formed by all functional and labor expenditures + government expenditures and large investments + Investments + the difference between imports and exports, (GDP = C + G + I + NX). This is a traditional form of the

US GDP equation. From GDP or total gross business, other derivatives and calculations and indicators of economic
success and reproduction cycles arise in the USA and
other countries. For example, the net income of the USA
for 2016 is 3.30 trillion dollars, which is significantly different from the gross domestic product and we recognize
it in the tax money that the IRS accumulates through tax
brackets from all taxpayers involved in creating the total
gross domestic product as from taxation procedures and
other revenues belonging to that group of taxpayers. The
goal of this federal government tax process is to define
the total number and total personal income of wage earners and corporations involved in GDP and to determine
their individual and collective contribution to net income
as individuals and to corporations, states, cities, and the
US as a whole. It is part of those calculations if they are
successful that indicate the growth and shift of the layer
of capital that we illustrated in our graphic Attachment
through a spiral, to a new higher level. Most often, the indicators of successful one-year operations for that part of
the visible indicators related to federal revenue are defined
by the equation:

Federation net income divided with GDP = rational ratio
of business performance (revenue ratio)

3.18 trillion dollars :(divided) by 18.620 trillion dollars =
0.17,4 We call this ratio, which we regularly show in all statistics from year to year, a rational ratio of the Federation's
income to GDP ratio, which, if it shows growth from year

to year, also shows successful business and vice versa, if it falls it shows unsuccessful business.

Net Federal revenue in 2016 was formed from:

- taxes on individual income	1.48 trillion dollars	47%
- salary taxes, payrolls	1.07 trillion dollars	33%
- corporate taxes	341 billion dollars	11%
- taxes on other earnings (miscellaneous)	156.6 billion dollars	5%
- taxes on cigarettes, alcohol and other (excise taxes)	95.9 billion dollars	3%
- duty	36.8 billion dollars	1%

The formation of 50 states government revenue uses the identical principle of net income generation and consists of the following sources:

- combination funds of the federation and the state	33.4%
- sale taxes	23.1%
- various funds and salaries	18.3%
- individual income taxes	18.0%
- other taxes	4.9%
- taxes from corporate income	2.0%

Displays and sources of income for corporate operations of all types of activities within GDP, both in the sphere of production of means of production and means of consumption and services within social activities and services of material production, financial institutions and others will not be shown in indicators that represent basic sources and resources which form the income of these corporations. We will illustrate this presentation with the well-known statement that every net profit of any corporation is regularly formed by an adequate amount of materialized human labor contained in the corporate means of production and live current work of the employees of these institutions.

If the relationship between the quantitative and qualitative quantity of current human labor within corporate operations is not in line with the needs of corporations, net profit or net income is regularly absent or insufficient. Just as we presented the revenue ratio of the US Federation in the formula: Federation Revenue Ratio = Federation Revenue: US GDP, it is possible to show other parts of US corporate business in some rational form that fits into that creative elliptical vortex and business performance of those corporations. In doing so, one cannot ignore the statement that even in the case of describing the sources of income of the Federation of the USA, whose deep historical foundations are related to the values of materialized past labor and live current labor, the creation of newly generated value stems from all available functional layers of wage earners live current work for each calendar year. Federal revenue, as we have shown in our sources, in 80% of cases is causally related to the layers of wage labor in all forms of corporate creativity in the USA. If we add to this corporate taxes and taxes on other royalties, we notice that net Federal revenue is tied exclusively to the live current work of all layers of American wage earners and citizens represented by their corporations and the GDP in which they participate in the calendar business year. Wage earners and corporate participation in Federal Revenue is regularly shown in tax brackets, corporate contribution is recognized by the amount of taxes that corporations are required to allocate from their gross income for Federal Revenue or income of a particular state and city to which the corporation gravitates or belongs. Just as the Federal Revenue is formed, the income of corporations, individuals and other institutions is formed, but no income of any type of corporation, including the income of financial institutions or stock markets, can bypass its basic foundations of direct income or transmission of income from the cycle of live current work of wage earners which forms a fundamental value creative starting point on which our income and annual business depend. Net income of corporations is formed according to the formula: corporate net profit = total sales - operating expenses.

In order to better understand the overall creative and self-creative wage earners position and its stratification in this whole systemic presentation of tax liabilities, we will use the presentation of IRS tax brackets for 2016 in which 141,200,000 million taxpayers form conditional and primarily "other's net" revenues, and only after that their own income. Most wage earners cannot legally enact a "law on the formation of one's own income" as can corporation bodies or state or federal authorities. The wage earners income of the largest part of the wage stratification is defined by institutions that are also owners or private owners of dominant capital or managers of legal accumulation of capital. Let us recall the determinant from the basic maxim that defines daily wage labor.

For further illustrations, we will use the presentation and description of the Attachment: 9.

Tax brackets in 2016 in which the percentage amounts that are the basis for taxation of wage earners are written on the left, followed by columns of different taxpayers and their earnings that belong to the percentage of taxes as indicated in the column. The final column of the contribution refers to the number of wage earners who belong to certain layers of wage earners for the year 2016.

Attachment: 9. Tax brackets 2016.

Tax bracket taxpayers total, 2016	Individuals	Married Couples together	Head of the family
0% 36,860,716			
10% 27,400,000	$0-$9275	$0-$18550	$0-$13,250
15% 42.000,000	$9276-$37650	$18,550-$75300	$13,250-$50,400
25% 24,009,141	$37,650-$91,150	$75,300-$151900	$50.400-$130,150
28% 4,603.602	$91,159-$190,150	$151,900-$231,450	$130,150-$210,800

33% 1,768.562	$190,150-$430,350	$231,450-$414350	$210,800-$413,350
35% 175,838	$413,350-$415,050	$413,350-466,950	$413,350-$441,000
39,6 % 892.420	$515,050 +	$466.950 +	$441,000 +

In the following, we will provide a statistical and percentage overview and a scale of the largest and smallest taxpayers in American society.

Attachment 9. Participation of tax brackets in the payment of all types of taxes in the USA (2015 data).

There are several data that stand out in the foreground from this presentation, namely that most taxes are paid by owners of larger amounts of income and secondly in all tax brackets there are "intermediate tax brackets", which are today called progressive tax brackets so that even the poorest and richest wage earners do not have to belong strictly to the tax bracket that defines the reported tax revenue at the outset. The share of wage earners with incomes of 0- $ 500k who participate in the tax procedure is 91%, which means that their work has invested by far the most time (time is money) to achieve not only their earnings but the entire GDP in the reproductive cycle of the USA. The share of rich ones reporting income amounts over $ 500 K is 9% and, within that 9%, as the table shows, only 0.8% are rich with income exceeding $ 2M.

Tax income	Share in population	Total participation in taxes	Average paid tax
$2 M	0.1%	20.4 %	27.5 %
$500K-2M	0.8%	17.9 %	26.8 %
$200K-500K	3.5%	20.6 %	19.4 %
$100K-200K	12,3%	21.7 %	12.7 %
$50K-100K	21.84%	14.1 %	9.2 %
$30K-50K	17,6 %	4.0 %	7.2 %
Less than $30K	43.8 %	1.4 %	4.9 %

In 2015, in addition to the basic tax brackets, about twenty intermediate tax brackets were offered, which are not shown in this Attachment 10 and serve as a progressive record of taxes of more complex forms of management in both individual income and salary income of wage earners or corporate taxpayers.

What is not visible not only in the formation of wage earning income but in the formation of net income of the federation, states and corporate profits is the origin of the net profit of all entities that form their income from the taxed value of wage earner labor and its market guaranteed value of labor controlled almost entirely by dominant capital. It seems that the wage earner works not only for the wage that belongs only to him in agreement with his employer, but also for the part of the wage that is cut and dictated by the society capital relation as a simultaneous source of net income of most social entities that are settled in their net income from those gross wage incomes which, although they do not belong to him, are recorded in his name.... We have already given an overview of the formation of federal net income, a sketch of the formation of state revenues, local governments (cities and megalopolises) and corporations, and it remains to record the net income of an individual wage earner if the wage earner manages to form it from the remaining taxable income that is personally his or belongs to his family or the partnership he prefers. A large proportion of lower-class wage earners generate income that has far more flow-through characteristics than income. Even if they form free net income, it is essentially in the process and function of the purposeful consumption of wider reproduction, which could not be said to be individual income in any economic calculation. Every owner of a corporation that is at the level of simple or reduced reproduction and stagnates with its results has similar income characteristics. This is as we know, especially if it has a long duration, for whatever reason, a devastating business orientation of a static nature. This static dictated form of income has been very well known to 40-45% of lower tax bracket wage earners for decades.

2019 TAX BRACKETS

In parallel, apart from the fact that each wage earner monitors his own income, his net income from the data of GDP, Federation, state, local government and corporations is monitored in his reach and potential by the dominant capital institutions, most often by analytical procedures of various federal agencies which are the companions and recorders of wage net income in its reach of supply and demand of the widest spectrum, within social participation in general. Generally, every employed wage earner not only creates his own net income but also the net income of a corporation, state federation or local community. His net income is the foundation of all social activities (education, healthcare, culture, science, etc.) but also all material activities of infrastructure and energy, both locally in urban and rural areas, and at the level of the state, federation or the world as a whole. The quantities that are monitored from the primary sources of production and consumption that are all around us and that are the focus of the functional characteristics of each wage earner are called CPI (Consumer Price Index) or basket of direct consumption of all wage earners. Many economists believe that the price basket is the most objective indicator of the overall state of economic success or failure of social communities. From the point of view and starting point of social participation, the basket is the first and basic reference point for the wage population from which the primary decisions about possible social participation grow. This CPI or price basket is essentially the last barrier that directs both quantitative and qualitative guidance to rationalize and define its net income. As we have already stated, for most wage earners, net income is rarely formed so that free capital is observed or recorded in it. The entire world economy is preoccupied with debts that essentially represent the anticipated and "realized income" guaranteed by world wage earners, so the position of world wage earners whose status is fully defined by legislation capitalized by dominant capital is defined as a debt part of economic calculations within all walks of life. We have already pointed out that the static properties of capital and capital relations and the starting value of the reproductive relations of production are shifted exclusively by the live current work of the wage earners of the world. However, it should be emphasized that an important condition of borrowing that allows anticipation of income for dominant capital is actually based on the status characteristics of wage capital, which in the processes of current work creates any newly created value and thus part of the value that covers debt obligations of dominant capital in the anticipated future. This process is present in the entire world creative and reproductive economy, which would not be possible without wage labor that is conditioned to create new value in existing capital relations. If we go back only briefly to the overview we presented in the previous text which indicates who forms the net income within GDP from the tax values of gross wage income generated from their current work in the USA (or anywhere in the world) we see the following entities: federation, states, cities and local government, corporations in the sphere of production of means of production and the sphere of production of means of consumption, as well as all other entities in daily consumption. We also notice the entire structure of the legal economic and political system, which significantly and exclusively depends on the value of current wage labor and income, whether we are talking about gross or net wage income, which is entirely intended for consumption and its social function. This is especially evident in the everyday economy in the sphere of material production, in which the economic concept in charge of investment policy is seen in the foreground, which, without wage labor, would be completely without a positive alternative. This investment-debt concept, which burdens GDP with debt repayment obligations within its own country or international economic, banking, and financial obligations and instruments, could not function without all the layers of wage labor that belong to it. The number of wage earners (in the USA 142-145,000,000 million on the tax lists in 2019) that the socio-political community of the USA has never or very rarely and indirectly participates in creating any economic policy, even the latest trends based on debt that exceeds the existing GDP. Only the upper strata of the tax brackets have, according to the sum of the possessions of dominant capital as private property, this possibility to plan, manage and define through legal instruments and institutions (Federal Reserve) with the reproductive system and its quantitative and qualitative functions. The number of wage earners in the USA is an essential basic foundation of stability in its economic policy and its reproductive cycles. Likewise, other countries of the world were those of capitalist or socialist political provenance and modern aspirations. The dominant capital of the most developed countries of the world also controls the number of employed wage earners around the world in other countries that make a profit of the parent companies of developed countries in both capitalist and socialist imperial policies around the world. As we see, the reach of the dictated (by dominant capital) creative current work of every wage earner in existing capital relations around the world does not begin its daily activity as a free creator but as a conditional debtor within the indebted reproductive community. Indebtedness is dictated by the nature of the dominant capital recognizable to every entrepreneur in the exponential commanding, imposed metaphysical force imposed by the dictates of the sums of capital in private and managerial possession of the upper strata (owners of capital) of wage strata of each society and protected by the legal system. A rational vision of change for all existing economic legal and political systems in a different social position and the functions of modern wage labor and wage earners themselves do not exist in the capitalist communities of the world or in the socialist communities we know today. Modern forms of capital relations represent the only and predetermined commitment that begins with the legal maxim that is the basic basis of social participation: "everything that a wage earner achieves for his employer within 8 hours of work belongs to the employer or capital owner." As the owner of capital has defined the entire instrument of social relations (rule of law) that helps him in this in the profiles of the legal, political, and economic system. The primary goal of the owner of the capital is to achieve the highest possible wage earners labor value of live current work, which elements the entire scope and reach of the social functions of maintaining the existing social reproduction. This is evident in the taxation procedures of wage earners, corporations, local governments, states and federations and the social system in general, which is a function of capital. Within the time we have defined as current work (8-16 hours per day), the wage earner is defined and planned by the dominant capital at the same time as his tax debt and contributions by taxes to other subjects of the legal, political and economic system we have mentioned. The spiral vortex and the growth of dominant capital is inconceivable without wage earners creative and creative participation, that is, wage live current work. The layers of wage earners that we present in our social functions through tax brackets only in their small part form the accumulation of free capital and profit from the value of current work of other layers of wage earners intended for the next cycles of reproductive management. The privileged position of wealthy wage earners from the upper strata of the tax brackets who own most of the accumulation of capital and profits has its source in the work of other wage earners and the legal system that defines each part of the social process of creating new value through wage creative live work, its social verification , consumption, and the recording of accumulation and profit, which very often becomes not only the personal income of the wage earning owners of dominant capital but also the source of their unlimited power in social participation through the legal economic and political system.

No wage earner, from neither lower nor higher classes of the tax brackets, neither as the owner of dominant capital nor as a mere wage earner, can or will, neither today nor in the future, reject the existing concept of creating new values, new accumulation, profit and capital. Judging by the indicators so far, the capitalist organization of the reproductive processes will not change anything in its essential features, neither now nor in the distant future. What is unsustainable in the existing creative spiral of gradual transition of the quantity of human achievements to the new quality is the undefined right of wage earners to participate in the management of their creative work and to discuss spending, investments, political power, international trade from the perspective of the creator of newly generated value which is constantly growing. This right in the immediate creative process is denied to most wage earners especially those who are in the lower places of the tax brackets. In future processes, in a rational and pragmatic practice intended for all participants in reproductive processes and new visions from the existing ones offered by the existing capital relations of private capital owners, human creators will have their say unencumbered by the dictates of private accumulation, profit and capital by a relationship that largely belongs only to the upper tax brackets of wage earners, which we usually illustrate with 0.1%, which is part of today's reality and everyday life. The quantity and quality of creative and self-creative work will grow over time and will outgrow the framework of the now dominant private capital, which will become the "tight skin" of the entire social reproductive system.

We will show what this means in concrete terms on the example of tax brackets used today (2019) on the basis of which wage taxation is realized again as in previous years, which also means the process of forming net income of federations, states, corporate cities and other social entities alimented financially by wage earners and their wage labor work USA through their tax money.

Attachment 10: 2019 tax brackets in the USA

Tax bracket	Individual taxes	Marr. couple together	Marr. couple separately	Head of the family
10%	$ 9,700	$0-19.400	$0-$9,700	$0-$13850
12 %	$9,701-$39,475	$19.401-$ 78.950	$9,701 $ 39,475	$13851 $52,850
22 %	$39,475 $84,200	$ 78,951 $ 168.400	$ 39,476 $ 84,200	$52,851 $84,200
24 %	$84,201 $160,725	$ 168.401 $321,450	$84,201 $160,725	$84,201 $160,700
32 %	$ 160,726 $204,100	$321,450 $408,200	$160,725 $204,100	$160,701 $204,100
35 %	$204,101 $510,300	$408,201 $612,350	$204,101 $306175	$204,101 $510,300
37 %	$510,301 and more	$612,351 and more	$306,176 and more	$510,301 and more

There is almost no difference between the amounts that are taxed and the percentage amount in tax brackets in 2016, which we presented earlier in Attachment 9, and this one, which is in force today in 2019, especially if we keep in mind that there are intermediate brackets in tax columns.

The existence of tax brackets and intermediate brackets used today serves to "more precisely and fairly" tax the wage labor. What we are interested in is certainly not only the tax formal legal mechanism that serves the private capital of capitalist or bureaucratic managers of social communities, but primarily those indicators that show the position of wage labor and the ratio of newly created wage earners value to conditions that raise both quantitative and qualitative social position of wage earners from all tax brackets to a higher level or their higher standard of living. The reduction of tax liabilities for corporations from 35% to 21% increased employment without at the same time noticing a significant shift in the personal income of wage earners, especially those at the lower end of the tax scale. This means: firstly, the growth of net income of individual wage earners has been stagnant for 60 years, the growth of net income of corporations is growing, thirdly, the net income of the federation, state, local government and all other entities that form their net income from tax gross income of the increased number of employed wage earners. The accumulation and profit of wage earners, private owners of dominant capital both within their own corporations with limited partnerships, those who sell their shares daily on the free stock markets around the world and especially financial institutions with a huge legal investment arsenal of private capital.

The reduction of taxes from 35% to 21% given by law to corporations is not reflected in the tax brackets intended to tax the net income of wage earners in the past two years as long as the law is in force, except in the part that represents wage earners owning capital of high tax brackets including managers of capital and capital ratio. It would be logical within each partnership to give each capital that is an entity within the reproduction cycles an equal stimulus that would result in increased accumulation and profits belonging to each capital if realized in the same reproduction cycle, including wage earners capital and wage net income without which social reproduction would be unthinkable. In such one-sided decisions noticeable in the application of tax reduction for corporations, dictated by the legally greedy nature of capital that we recognize in the legal political and economic system, which overwhelm our modern egoistic consciousness, this partnership equivalence is not present nor are legal instruments given to correct or supplement that decision. In these circumstances and such a practice that favors private dominant capital, the overall rational and independent scope of the decision of the US Congress and Senate that defines the economic relations of these benefits to other parts of capital within the process of creating GDP is not visible, especially when it comes to capital spent on labor market for all layers of wage earners who will unconditionally fertilize this 14% tax reduction benefit in the next reproduction processes in favor of corporate private capital and all other entities that will generate their net income from the quantitative qualitative inflow of newly created value of wage earners not owning larger amounts of dominant capital through tax money. Money as capital has endless alternatives, but its owner regularly nurtures only those that are the source of its accumulation and profit. Almost all analyzes of the growth of net wage income in the USA in the last 60 years show minimal growth of net income accumulation and relative stagnation of income, especially that of lower tax bracket wage earners. It is not our goal to look at other typed inequalities in the acquisition of individual income related to race, gender, the impact of technical and technological applications, globalization, that significantly affect employment and the amount of wages of wage earners or capital in general. With this review, illustrated with the circumstances that are noticeable in the legal political and above all economic system in the USA with the reduction of tax corporations by 14%, we wanted to emphasize the static ratio of legal capital to the net income of US wage earners and their direct contribution to the growth of newly created values and accumulation of income of all participants within the reproductive processes. The entire legal, political, and economic system of the United States seems to have accepted this as normal practice and is satisfied with indicators that show that the growth of most wage earnings is left to grow solely by an exhausting amount of work over time. The growth in the amount of labor, as in this case, neglects the growth in the quality of wage earners capital and one's personal income after taxing their net income. We single out another very important feature of the egoistic nature of capital and capital relations that characterizes us in our social relations, and that is that there is no capital for any capital or other guarantor of survival and fertilization, but only work and creative wage labor. The results of wage labor are the basis of any GDP or any net income formed from the tax money of wage earners in each country. This is especially evident in circumstances of economic recessions or natural cataclysms when due to bad business or some other reason formal legal actions of capital owners that create a new stable economic balance always and primarily resort to cheap and easily dictated wage earners labor that guarantees newly created values from their current wage labor, without which capitalism or socialism would not be possible. There are no other sources for modern GDP or for anyone's net income within social communities. Of course, tax brackets are a mirror of the national distribution of newly created value and in their form, we recognize the basic legal, correct or less correct features of successful business but also the standard of social cohesion and stability of communities in the world. This legal mechanism defines personal freedom and creativity of every wage earner.

The nature of the dictate and hierarchy of capital and capital relations from the highest to the lowest level indicates the regular antagonism and intolerance of larger capital towards smaller ones especially if smaller capital grows independently of the surrounding capital. Larger capital does not suffer the growth of smaller amounts of capital unless they are strictly controlled in their reach and power. In this regard, we emphasize the dictated position of wage capital or its impact on the existing establishment and "rule of law and law order", or the implementation of law in the world which, on the scale of legal hierarchical values we know today, ensures primarily the position and functional reproductive status of the largest dominant capital of the social community on the top of the scale. This capital dominates in its relative independence and does not want changes that cannot be controlled by the legal, political or economic system, which is constantly monitored by the reproductive functions of all strata and the functions of social communities, especially the function of wage production and consumption which is exclusively conditioned by the dictates of reproductive laws to create constantly new and greater value.

The forces of influence of the wage-earner population around the world are inconceivable and completely unused. The whole reality of the capital relation in which the functions of the creative work of wage earners (David as creative work) and the accumulation of capital (Goliath as accumulation of dominant capital in private ownership) are constantly intertwined is like a balance of power between David and Goliath, which also announces the final swing of David's slingshot and the emergence of a new creative history of (wage earners) free creators without the capital relations of the private capital of owners and smaller ownership groups that identified with the powerful sums of capital appropriated from the labor of others. On the other hand, the daily current creative work of wage earners, despite being controlled by the dictates of wages cut by dominant capital, is the only regular contribution to historical shifts from lower quantitative and qualitative creations to higher quantitative and qualitative forms of creativity in all fields where human labor is present. There are actually no other forms of quantitative and qualitative shifts in our human practice and historical development. Existing capital relationship in this creative current work is only a necessary static process pendant installed to control the growth of legally protected egoism of private possession of capital and the dictates of capital itself. Capital, together with the predispositions of current earners wage work, is the starting point of new reproductive creations, also generated in the earlier processes of the past live current work of wage earners. The social relation or capital relation that we know today is in its planned features and realization regularly marked by the time required for the planned reproductive realization and production creation. The price of an hour of current work of wage earners varies from one corporation to another and we can calculate and present it as the average price of an hour of work of an individual, corporation, state and federation, and even the world. All these data are defined by the existing capital and capital relation, and what does not exist within the calculations of capital and capital relations is the quantitative and qualitative feature and price of creation itself together with the necessary time of work that is rationally and creatively possessed exclusively by the creative wage earner. These properties of the value of creative labor are completely unknown in the characteristics and amounts of capital, although due to the dictates of wage labor prices they belong to it and appear in surplus value, profit and accumulation of owners of dominant capital and are actually its creators. To illustrate the relationship between private owners of accumulation and capital and wage labor is like a breakfast buffet from which it is possible to satisfy both quantitative and qualitative needs regardless of information about the creator of the buffet and its contents.

Attachment 11: Availability of basic social standards of capital relations according to indicators of modern practice

Basic taxation of wage earners in 2019 year in USA and influence of wage earner's capital on possession and availability of existing values of capital relations in USA society:

Wage earner's Tax Brackets	Forming new private Capital	Starting private LLC	Influence on election program	High standard of leaving	Influence on law politic and economy	capacity to influence information. systems	Affordability of good Education	Affordability of good health insurance	0%-100%
37%, More than $ 500,000 dollars 0,1% population									
35 % not more than $ 500,000 dollars 0,8% population									
32% not more then $ 200,000 dollars 3,5% population									
24% no more than $157,000 dollars 12,3 % population									
22%no more than $ 82,500 dollars 21,84% population									
12% no more than $ 38,700 dollars 17,6 % population									
10% no more than $ 9525 dollars 43.8 % population 0%									

Through the illustration provided by this attachment, I want to acquaint the reader with the trends that are evident in our everyday social life, which are based on capital that we as wage earners create and own every day as private equity or as capital owned by others for which we also create as wage earners. The difference between private ownership of capital and capital relations and the function of capital as social property that we find in state capitalism and socialist communities does not exist or is insignificant and state capitalism and socialism can coexist in existing conditions only if it can be in the function of everyday models of capital relations and we know today. Our goal is to point out that both accumulation and capital will eventually be realized in the form of non-proprietary social relations that will support the newly formed creative and self-creative consciousness of all layers of wage earners. The processes of continuous current work are yet to come in the form of constant rational creativity of all wage earners who will not have a dominant capital orientation but a newly created pragmatic and functional value that does not need ownership attributes. Under the constant development of qualitative and quantitative values of wage labor in all fields, ownership will become an increasingly rational vision of the right and duty to work and create, which will be distributed through developed and open information systems to non-private property, and to every creative and self-creative individual or every creative entity in a universally organized reproduction function. This essentially refers to a legal form of not private or social ownership but to non-proprietary social relations. In this regard, this diagram illustrates the contemporary process and scope of our current individual predispositions based on own and other available private capital in co-ownership and private ownership partnerships. The whole diagram represents the layers of wage earners taxed by the American legal system (or any other capital relations system) as we see painted with layers of colors that imperceptibly permeate in watercolor style and merge into the landscape horizon of the wage society in which we live. The layers of wage earners are visible on the left side of the diagram and follow the layers of colors in the landscape height. At the top is a strong red color that represents the wage strata of the highest earnings including the richest individuals of American society who make up 0.1% of the population. It is also noticed that the red color fades towards the lower strata on the scale and towards the wage earnings with lower annual earnings. The intention of this art diagram is to point out to the reader the trends and scope not only of the monetary value of annual income but also of reaching one's own individual power based on that value in the existing social capital relation we form with other wage earners in which live in each new reproductive cycle. Therefore, on the right side of the landscape diagram we have added a percentage scale of 0% -100% expressed in color as well as to the diagram followed by the range of availability of marked goals at the top of the landscape diagram that everyone in the wage population wants to achieve, which are an integral part of the general dictate of capital and the capital relations in which we as historical beings are placed voluntarily or violently. There are no other more precise research designations in this diagram. There are two reasons for this a) first, exact comparative qualitative and quantitative surveys of wage status have not been conducted for this book, although they are known in many studies by other authors (only partially mentioned in this book) and b) second reason, this diagram makes sense to be a methodological guide to every reader, which should be useful in understanding one's own and others' wage social functions with which individuals and layers of wage earners participate daily in social capital relations not only in American society and not only in capitalism but also in socialist communities around the world. In this regard, we will begin by commenting on the columns in Attachment 11, which indicate only some of the goals and basic conditions of wage creative life and work.

"Formation of a new dominant capital" is the title and wage earners goal of the first column that we are working on first. In the current evaluation of human wage labor and in existing legal systems around the world and in the USA, and according to data that are an integral part of the basic characteristics of corporate wage income recorded and used in the reproductive cycle to form local or city, state and federal income, very little of the free money remains available to lower-income wage earners and it is almost certain that these wage earners do not have free investment capital to invest in their own new corporation or in another corporation as partners, or in the stock market. Their investment social participation, which we quantify with percentage marks on the diagram from 0% to 100%, is reduced only to the part of our own income that we can mark in 0% of investment predispositions intended for the formation of our own corporation. The reason for such a situation is defined by the general status functions of a part of the wage earners capital and with it a good part of the wage earners in reproductive cycles. Almost all the wages of lower-class wage earners are spent on the "basket" and the primary cost of living for individuals and families. Higher layers of wage earners tax brackets, starting at $ 200,000 and up, indicate an excess of unspent capital that in cases such as Amazon's owner J. Bezos climbs to fantastic sums of both private personal income and the income of corporations owned by those wage earning capital owners, which we mentioned earlier. Income from higher tax brackets opens investment doors everywhere both within home countries and outside those countries around the world. We emphasize that capital does not need a passport or visa anywhere in the world. Regardless of customs restrictions and indicators of the ratio of imports and exports in the balance sheets of countries around the world, free investment capital is regularly realized in various forms and balanced relations between investors and recipients of investment capital. If the world economy lost this balanced predisposition for the placement of capital in the existing capital relations of the world economy (and not only financial capital), the world would turn into a statically extensive closed-type economy.

We skip the second column of the diagram and go to the third column of Attachment 11. "Influence on the electoral (election) program" and the goals of democratic development of communities is a significant or perhaps, in addition to creating capital through creative current work, one of the most significant creative functions of the daily current work of modern wage earners around the world. Judging by the usual practice of the election process, all taxpayers on our scale have the right to participate in the election process defined primarily by the program campaign of candidates, both individuals and the Democratic and Republican parties or any other party, based on capital and capital relations controlled and possessed by them. Of course, the most numerous layers of lower tax brackets cannot collect large enough sums of capital for their independent influence in the election process, neither from their own sources nor from other sources of earmarked or free capital in those layers because it does not exist in those layers. It is to be assumed that investment capital owners very rarely fund typical programs and resolutions of the poor wage classes. There is always the possibility that a candidate, individual or group will be accepted by their program in the dominant party resolutions and election procedure if it is apologetically written in its favor or in favor of capital and capital relations. The wage number of the lower wage brackets is its greatest strength and influence on creative participation in the quantitative number of pre-election procedures and in the final voting. Presentation of precise resolutions of parties and party candidates that will be realized if winning the elections is not a common practice in modern election procedure and the campaign is usually reduced to political marketing based on pragmatism, capital relations of popular republican or democratic parties, without firm guidelines that define changes in advance which is caused by the position and amount of capital that political parties have or want to manage. Everything is conditioned by the dictate of capital. The dictatorship of capital conditions every political procedure, even elections. Even the smallest changes observed as a result of political campaigns and changes are not acceptable in the form of automatism and if they are to be implemented in political practice in the existing legal system, they must be fought for not only by a political campaign but by real capital owned by a political current or party which strives for changes and which dominates in practice. The spillover of capital into a new common practice unknown form of capital and capital relations or into a new democratic form of state or social ownership is mostly dominant legal private equity which is dominated by unacceptable and often inconceivable procedure regardless of the model's abundance of democratic and public benefit progress. New creative democratic procedures are exceedingly rare and poor in progressive solutions both in the electoral process and in the changes that these electoral winners bring in their new practice. Capitalist democracy has for centuries been a static conservative and persistent form of government dictated and marked by fear of the survival of private capital and capital relations that has maintained it in the existing known principles of equality, brotherhood and freedom since the Dutch, English, French and American bourgeois revolutions although the practice of capital development in modern trends records and offers many different indicators and possibilities. Unlike capitalist democracy, socialism is also defined by the dictates of capital and capital relations governed by bureaucrats and party elites in power. The practice for most wage earners is the same in both capitalism and socialism, only the taxation of wage earners in their characteristics is of a different order. Socialist wage earners in their final personal income (monthly salary) are "exempt" from paying taxes. Almost every part of material costs and depreciation of income and allocations from income for social activities or activities of material production and allocations from the net income of labor organizations (or socialist corporations) of socialism for personal income and local needs as well as in capitalism has its sources in wage labor. Both the wage earners of capitalism and the wage earners of socialism maintain their social systems a capital relation with the value of their creative and self-creative work that forms accumulation, capital, and profit. As long as there is capital and capital relation as a general culture of economics and as a basic social feature of human socialization, historical currents of social movements will not create an abundance of new progressive platforms nor will the dynamics of significant changes in the dictates of capital that mark us change. The overall democratic reality of the modern world is extremely static and politically and democratically uncreative, which will certainly change the future of creative current work if all-round creative human wage labor is to be an independent (from private capital and bureaucratic forms of government and disposal of capital) creative factor. This is especially important because of private-equity capitalist discipline and control of creative current wage labor that limits the vast resources of human current creative labor and the right to use inheritance in forms of past labor in limited reproductive practice sufficient only for concepts of private equity dominant capital. However, the layer of capital is still shifting, and the horizons of creativity are unstoppably expanding with constant live current work, as we have outlined in Attachment 6.

"Influence on the election program". Two approaches to this issue are regularly relevant. First, the impact on the voting population and the entire election process that an ambitious candidate can have together with the support of his/her political party for a period of two, four years or more or permanently appropriate political marketing. Second, the particular and singular reflection and impact on the electoral population modified by the election campaign on election day itself. In the last few voting years in the USA, which are held every four years, 61% of voters with American citizenship have been active. We represented this population in the wage strata of taxpayers according to the classes to which they belong as well as their family members with the right to vote in the American election process. Minority groups of citizens of different ethnicities, as well as the layers of wage earners with the lowest incomes and possession of capital, are also inactive in the electoral process.

From the wage strata from the existing tax brackets showing the wage strata in our case in the USA, who can be the president of the US. The primary constitutional answer to this question is that in an American democracy, any citizen or wage earner can be president. In the pragmatic practice of American everyday life, however, things are different. Most American wage earners do not even think about their realistic placement in the campaign for president, senator, congressman in federal state or local city parliamentary bodies... One of the important reasons, especially for the wage earners of the lower parts of the tax brackets, is that they are not the owners of capital to ensure their political engagement in the parties they opt for, but also electoral participation and independence both during the election process and in expenses, unlike the upper layers of tax brackets where richer citizens belong to whom electoral participation is more accessible as regularly shown by the population of 0.1% of billionaires who can directly enter the electoral process "by buying the basic conditions" of electoral participation without being proposed in a different and more appropriate political electoral way. An exceptional and modern example of the participation of the rich in the pre-election procedure of the Democratic Party to nominate a candidate for the presidency of the USA, although unsuccessful, happened in the election procedure in 2019-2020. Mike Bloomberg, a successful businessman and philanthropist who spent about $ 220,000,000 million by January 2020 alone, was also involved in the election campaign. Mike Bloomberg relentlessly spent his money on the Internet and online videos, degrading incumbent President Donald Trump, who should be an opponent of the new Democratic candidate in the 2020 election. Mike Bloomberg also spends his money on forming new groups of voters, election marketing and many other activities that a conscientious participant in the presidential election process must direct and organize in order to take place. As announced from Mike Bloomberg's staff during his participation, he was ready to spend a billion dollars in his election procedure and candidacy to defeat the Republican candidate Donald Trump. Those sums of money are inaccessible even to the best candidates of democratic platforms and resolutions behind which stands the wider democratic population. The budget of other Democratic Party candidates is much smaller, which does not diminish their chances in the final voting process and defining the main candidate within the Democratic Party of the USA, which will eventually have to choose only one candidate to fight the Republican President Donald Trump in 2020.

Quantitative and qualitative analyzes of not only these goals and commitments presented in our diagram (Attachment 11) and the columns we present but also many other goals that wage earners have can provide a reference result of mean values that would define for each wage earner and the tax bracket to which he belongs social participation through the corresponding strength or weakness expressed by the percentage of availability (in relation to the goal) which in the existing capital relation is expressed as a participant in the reproductive cycles. The overall notion of the distribution of social power arising from capital held within wage strata (individuals and total) essentially defines the pulsating meaning of the existing capital re-lations of the communities to which we belong but also of each wage earners class and individuals separately. Complex sociological analyzes of this social feature that we advocate are not common, but if they were worthwhile, they would have an idea of the basic features that can be considered as the basis for changes in the political, legal and economic system. Unfortunately, the world reality and the legal events of the primary decision on everything are made by the dominant private capital in the possession of the upper wage earners classes directly or indirectly, which is also the holder of the primary right to dispose of capital and general capital relations of social communities. There is no legal boundary between less affluent owners of capital and owners of dominant capital. It is an imaginary Rubicon that is defined and becomes recognizable by the growth of capital owned by the middle strata of the wage earners population, which tends to grow towards larger amounts or dominant capital. Once this Rubicon is spun and this is possible only with the exploitation of other people's labor and when a group or individual becomes part of the dominant capital as the owner or co-owner of domestic or foreign multinational corporations, banks, natural resources and energy resources, huge units of information memory software and hardware basis of everyday capital relation, science and other essential conditions of maintaining capital dominance, the private owner of capital whom we also call the rich wage earner of private capital becomes definitely the apologist of capitalism and capital relations. Being the owner of dominant capital within modern capitalism and the capital of returns based on the legal system intended for the duration of capitalist social relations also means that the company does not have a principled legal system with a permanent systemic code of ethics, which often means that expert court arbitrations platform of everyday success. The absolute majority of modern legal laws that use capital and capital relations is ambivalent and vague and regularly ends in favor of capital and its owners through arbitration. It is generally recognized that the legal system of modern capitalism used by capital in its subordinated relations, which ensures its emergence and accumulation within creative wage earners participations, is marked by far more "principled" and operational features that capital uses in the dictates of social reproductions and that the legal system of capitalism is equally much more legal and open to arbitration in that part of social reproduction which is related to the insignificant influence of the wage earners population on capital and capital relation with the right to participate in the democratic system of modern capitalist communities. The rule of law that controls our overall social participation is subordinate to existing capital and capital relations and there are essentially no significant improvements in the legal system that are aimed at improving and abolishing the dictate of capital. It is especially noticeable that there is no political initiative of legal changes based on the indicators of positive creative practice that precedes and gives the possibility of the emergence of these initiatives in order to improve it with each new creative reproductive cycle. Total world capitalism and its conservative features related to the basic principles of the dictates of capital and capital relations, described in the capitalist-socialist constitutions around the world, do not change. They are changed only by the creative and self-creative wage-earning current work of all layers of wage earners who, both in the course of their current work and in materialized past work, leave an abundance of values that make them independent of the dictates of capital.

RESULTANT

Even these partial answers in several columns in Attachment 11, give a hint of the meaning of the resultant availability of certain values of capital relations that are to be achieved and which are indicated to the wage earners of different tax layers.

Attachment 11 A: availability of standards with percentage resultant R

Basic taxation of wage earners in 2019 year in USA and influence of wage earner's capital on possession and availability of existing values of capital relations in USA society:

Wage earner's Tax Brackets	Forming new private Capital	Starting private LLC	Influence on election program	High standard of leaving	Influence on law politic and economy	capacity to influence information systems	Affordability of good Education	Affordability of good health insurance	0%-100% R
37%, More than $ 500,000 dollars 0,1% population	100 %				100 %			100 %	100 %
35 % not more than $ 500,000 dollars 0,8% population	90 %				90 %			90 %	90 %
32% not more then $ 200,000 dollars 3,5% population	70 %				75 %			80 %	75 %
24% no more than $157,000 dollars 12,3 % population	60 %				60 %			60 %	60 %
22%no more than $ 82,500 dollars 21,84% population	35 %				40 %			45 %	40 %
12% no more than $ 38,700 dollars 17,6 % population	20 %				20 %			25 %	21 %
10% no more than $ 9525 dollars 43.8 % population	5 %				5 %			5 %	5 %
0%	0 %				0 %			0 %	0 %

The resultant in our diagram is the sum of percentage values of 0-100% (in the diagram marked with R which is expressed by the sum of the average percentage availability of the capital ratio standard for the tax bracket. In our

Boro Stipanovic

article it can be seen that the largest part of the population of lower-class wage earners with a share in the population of 21.84%, 17.6% and 43.8% shown in three columns has a result of 40%, 21%, 5% availability of standards. In other words, the share in the population of these three tax layers of wages is 82.6% of the total population with the percentage availability expressed for three standards of 22%. The rest of the wage earners with significantly higher earnings belonging to the upper tax brackets are represented with their share in the population of 17.3% with 81% availability compared to the targets of these columns. The methodological approach of these analyzes is very illustrative both in the vertical analysis and in the horizontal indicators and the result itself, which is indicated for a particular wage tax layer. Just as the consumer price index (CPI) is used for primary consumption, there should be monitoring of the broader social standard of wage participation in various spheres of social life available from the perspective of private capital ownership that belongs to certain layers of wage earners. In this way, within the range between the highest and lowest capital holdings of individual layers of wage earners, which we present in tax brackets, a much more precise definition of the dynamics and reach of individual and social values could be obtained for each layer of wage earners separately based on the growth of general wage standards. The cycle of capital growth and accumulation in the reproductive cycles should not unreasonably leave anyone who participates in it with his work contribution unawarded, as the Trump administration did in the case of reducing the tax liabilities of American corporations (this was the strategy of other administrations before D. Trump and the practice that we often see in the rest of the modern capitalist world) with American wage earners, especially lower wage earners that are employees of these same corporations, which will, by dictate, now for 14% of increased capital corporations again create even more capital or accumulation of private capital owners to local governments, US states, the US Federation and banking and financial institutions for the same or slightly increased wages.

It is estimated that the dominant capital of the tax population of 0.1% in the USA increased by a 14% tax write-off for US corporations increased by more than 1 trillion dollars (within the GDP of 20 trillion dollars for the USA in 2019) which is an enormous sum which further deepens the gap between the upper and lower strata of wage earners without the possession of free investment capital. This also means that the dictates of increased capital will impose even greater obligations on the employed wage population in order to maintain it at the level it has reached. The reason why wages of personal wage earners stagnate is the necessary distance that the dictates of capital create between themselves and the wage earners and on behalf of the owner of capital so that they can continue to manage the dependent wage earning population in a new reproductive cycle. Capital owners in such circumstances rub their hands with satisfaction which is understandable from their perspective although not positive for the whole democratic practice. Political parties and parliamentary agencies are silent. The most common reason for not reacting is that there is no law in the existing legal system (rule of law), nor are such laws enacted, which protect the legal position and commitment that all wage earners involved in the US reproduction process (and in the world of developed capitalism) whether rich or poor or on the lower parts of the tax scale or the upper ones together should have a reciprocal attitude towards profit and tax values, as well as wage-earners owning capital if they are partners in creative reproductive processes.

This means that, for example, a tax payer in the lowest tax bracket of 10% on the amount of annual salary up to $ 9525 should also have a 14% tax write-off (cut of) as well as corporations, which in this particular case means that as long as this law lasts, the local government, the state and the federation should return 14% of $ 9524 earnings each year.

Regardless of the fact that such taxpayer does not have a corporation in the formal sense as in real practice, he is exposed in the existing socio-economic system to the same experiences as owners or co-owners of capital and corporations in the 0.1% tax bracket to which American and world's wealthiest people belong. A significant difference between the owner of a private personal capital that is both a co-owner of corporate capital and an owner who owns exclusively personal income as capital strictly intended for conditional consumption, is that the owner of personal capital and corporate capital conditions the owner of personal capital to work unconditionally for precisely controlled market value in another corporation. Both owners we present belong to the categories of wage earners (employee of dominant capital) subordinated to the actual realized but also abstract planned value of singular, particular and universal common capital (GDP), which must be achieved in reproductive cycles through the current work of all wage earners. To return to our initial maxim that defines a wage earner within a corporation as a creator whose labor value elements the agreed wage (as their personal income that is taxed and allocated to the local government, state, and federation) while the rest of the wage labor belongs to the corporate business owner that is equally taxed applying the tax rules for corporate business. Both the owner and co-owners of the corporate business are wage earners and as wage earners form personal income and corporate income which necessarily contains a new dictate of capital intended for new reproduction cycles in which all employed wage earners who are not owners or co-owners of corporate business and owners and co-owners of corporate business as wage earners participate. Together, through their creative work, they form their own personal income, but also the income of corporations whose contractors, owners, or co-owners they are. The owner and wage earner of the corporate business also plans other costs of corporate reproduction business as well.

This is also done by a wage earner who is not the owner or co-owner of a corporation only within the minimum reach of his personal income within his civic obligations. The entire reproductive cycle is dominated by the multi-layered dictate of capital of various legal obligations that we recognize only in tax layers as a feature of common social practice that primarily arises from the planned and dictated value of general social capital growth to which all are subordinated. Owners of universal, particular, and singular capital, regardless of where their capital is fertilized through wage labor, are given the tools of unconditional dictate with which the entire wage population is conditioned to work for a market wage. Without the conditioned dictates of capital that govern different rules, the creation of new social value, wage creative work, all social systems that use the dictate of capital and capital relations in their fundamental character (capitalism, socialism) could not survive today.

WHAT IS DOMINANT CAPITAL

Dominant capital is, for the most part, the newly created new value of the current work of market wage earners. Although in our text we have classified all taxpayers as wage earners in relation to the goal set and dictated by the total capital of the company, it is important to emphasize that among wage earners there is a difference in the privilege of capital accumulation and profit guaranteed by the legal system from the current work of all wage earners and those who are the possessors of capital and those who are not, within social reproduction.

The difference arises when a better and more creative wage earner who is also better rewarded for his work and thus gets the opportunity to employ one, two, three or a much larger number of market workers as a richer wage earner to maximize within the legal system (used for millennia as a legal common or legal basis for the creation of private capital) the work on the realization of his private goals within smaller or larger corporations domestically or worldwide as far as the possibilities of his capital in existing capital relations that may be the same or different from the original. The emergence of free money capital and its accumulation from the wage labor of a large number of creators shows the transition of the quantity of wage labor to a new quality in the form of profit or free money accumulated by one private owner, several co-owners, local government or state. There are of course other forms of profit that have no origin in creative human work based on the appropriation of natural resources of this planet into private possession by force. Legalization of ownership of part of the planet or the planet and beyond is one of the most shameless absurdities of modern legal law humanity benefits. The essential meaning of modern globalization is primarily focused on the complete control of wage earners creation, which regenerates ever new and always increased sums of accumulation and capital for the parent dominant capital. It could be stated that on the scale of taxpayers we recognize in the same group those wage earners who create accumulation and capital and those who, in addition to creating accumulation and capital, have the right to appropriate that same capital in the form of private ownership or other managerial bureaucratic possession. In this way, the part of wage earners that appropriates the largest part of the total accumulation, capital and profit created by the current work of all wage earners become both dominant protagonists and managers of social reproductions, as well as the basis of accumulation and capital of individuals, groups or today corporate business in general and capitalism and socialism. Its presence in practice and its basic significance is that it indisputably and universally indicates that only in these circumstances can labor be used to create smaller or larger sums of new accumulation and capital (profit) that become, because thru "rule of law" allows it, legal, private or social ownership. With these sums, wage earners creative and self-creative current labor is again dominated in a new expanded reproductive socio-economic cycle or capital relation. Precisely because of the realized accumulation and new capital appropriated in the private possession of the wage earners-owner of capital from multiplied wage earners labor, his wage-earning ownership function over accumulation and capital turns into a necessary organized creative dictate of multiplying and increasing existing accumulation and capital not only on the processes of creative work in the sphere of material production and consumption but also in the sphere of creating funds for consumption and society as a whole. The created capital, which always demands its increase from its existing values, is the Damocles sword of the entire history and especially the dynamics of today's corporate economy. Unfortunately, humanity has never had any other processes than the failed attempts to realize the social reproduction that creates accumulation and capital, nor does it know or use today. In today's corporate economy, we define corporate income in different bookkeeping and accounting ways. What these accounts have in common is that net profit or newly created net capital is the remainder after all corporation operating costs and benefits for various social obligations and functions have been settled by the law (rule of law). Within the creative and self-creative current wage earners work in the corporations themselves, a whole series of activities and creative work is primarily realized, which significantly affects the creation of newly created value and accumulation and capital of these corporations. Modern bookkeeping and accounting most often present every human work as a consumption of capital, not as a process of creating new value, and the resulting newly created value is recorded as the profit of the corporation without mentioning its wage earner. Here are just a few factors that are claimed to influence the creation of net profit or the rest of the financial capital that is the backbone of future cycles of expanded reproduction, without which it is impossible to keep corporations on an upward creative trajectory. Internal factors affecting profit are the following: a) trade efficiency, b) improving the quality of goods, c) increasing production, d) reducing production costs e) rational use of production capacity f) work on expanding the range, g) marketing..... Here are some external factors that corporation owners cannot be significantly affected by: a) location of the corporation (good or bad) b) environmental conditions and nature, c) support of local and state authorities, d) political situation in the country and the world, e) characteristics of the country's and world economy, f) transport and other external conditions beyond the control of the corporation. This is only a small part of the whole apologetic arsenal of economic scholasticism that is offered for use in modern economies of both capitalism and socialism of the world.

As can be seen, all these internal and external factors that create essential conditions for the accumulation of net financial capital essentially define the wage earners creation of new value, the price of newly created value of human past labor which will be converted into amounts of money to cover production costs and social obligations and finally define the balance we call profit or net financial gain that will belong to a corporation or private owner. What is also visible is that it is not recorded anywhere nor is it quantitatively or qualitatively processed as an active subject of creating new value by the creator of the newly created value, which in this discussion we call the wage earner and taxpayer. That is why we emphasize that the newly created use value of the created goods as well as its final turnover value is always the sum of the newly created values not only of the costs of wage labor but also of his creative work invested in it. As human creative wage labor is the only one that creates new value and use and turnover for the owner of capital is a market cost (not as partner capital), so it is recorded in corporate accounting items and accounting. Human creative work of wage earners in corporate business today is not perceived as a source of newly created both use and turnover value. The reason for this is primarily that modern corporate entrepreneur-ship and the most developed countries in the world do not have the benevolent legal partnership tools to evaluate the creative results of wage workers as a whole reproduction process from the beginning of the creative cycle, in fact, from the market where every wage earner appears and of-fers as free capital to his ultimate creative realization in the creative processes of corporations where the market value of products is realized, with which he would ensure the direct right to wage earners participation in profit. Such an approach to the wage population does not exist in practice nor is it touched upon by modern capitalist and socialist practice in its conceptions of the future. It is not visible in corporate practice and legal systems of the capital of the community in which this way human wage earners labor could rise from the level of a mere creative means (for the capitalist available on the market) to the level of a respected creative partnership that really belongs to it. The distribution of profits in today's capital relations and participation in the distribution of net money capital is available to wage earners only through shares on the mar-ket if they bought them earlier and if they were available in their market price for a suitable wage earners pocket. Many corporations do not have shares in the market and the money capital of such corporations belongs either only to the owner or the narrow circle of management and not to other employees of the corporation. In such corporations, wage earners are literally mere disenfranchised market wage earners without any opportunity to participate in the distribution of the newly created value they have created through their current work. Even in circumstances when there is an abundance of shares on the stock market that are offered for free sale at reasonable prices, according to indicators that show the possession of money visible in the tax brackets to which wage earners belong, there is a very small number of wage earners, especially in lower tax brackets, who have the opportunity to buy significant amounts of shares for the simple reason that, with their modest wage earnings, they have moved away from that possibility due to priority costs of another kind. Thus, a model and legality can be observed which indicates that although all wage earners participate in each phase of newly created value through their current work, the profit or net capital of corporations that remains at the end of the work cycle is available only to part of wage earners, pre-cisely those who invest the money capital in the variable and constant capital of the corporation and thus acquire the right to appropriate the full value of money capital, although it mostly belongs in origin to wage earners who, before the production process, did not have money capital to buy shares or other financial partnerships but, by their creative and self-creative work, participated in its creation as paid market wage earners. In order to clarify and com-plete the idea of the distribution of the part of benefits that we often see as belonging to corporate wage earners, we point out that in addition to shareholder dividends (if they own shares), wage earners sometimes receive a bonus de-fined as a special amount of money (which is most often formed after a determined profit) intended by the owner of capital or management to reward wage earners, or as a sum that partially complements the 401 K fund that American workers form in their corporations as a separate own pension fund, that is, savings. Money for bonuses and 401k do not belong to the net profit but are replenished from the wage compensation fund to the wage earner and are shown as an expense in corporate operations. Such and similar wage supplements should not be compared to net profit or cash capital primarily because profit is a new unspent amount of money generated after the successful creative reproduction of all wage earners who are employees of the corporation. Profit shows a new net accumulation of total past work of wage earners which, if invested (in part or in full) in the future expansion of the corporation's capacity, guarantees the successful reproduction and growth of the entire socio-political legal and primarily economic system. A wage earner who owns the capital of a corporation, unlike an ordinary market wage earner, in addition to shares, makes a net profit and returns capital from operations and earnings of his corporation on which he does not pay taxes because they are paid from the corporation's funds.

Of course, the non-participation of wage earners in the distribution of accumulated profits is an extreme injustice that society demonstrates to market wage earners, primarily because if you are a wage earner paid in the labor market without your own financial capital, you are informed that you are a means or tools dictated to realize at the same time your own creative ambitions, but also the creative intentions of another person (capital owner) who buys you on the market and pays you as a wage earner. Second, your wage-earning psychophysical being is conditioned by the dictates of capital and its owner to necessarily accept the market value of compensation for your work no matter what the real creative value of your current work is and your contribution to the newly created use and turnover value. Third, even though you, as a wage earner, are an active creator of newly created value through your past and live current work, if you are denied an equivalent partnership to share the profits you have made through the legal system, you also become a second-class citizen. At the same time, it is pointed out that only those wage earners who possess significant sums of equity with which they can actively participate in investing in their own corporation or shares of other corporations become, according to the amount of capital they own, respected citizens who participate in modern democratic forms of socio-political life. Fourth, the dictates of financial capital and capital relations in the labor market most often indicate that wage earners cannot influence the growth of their wages. The fifth legacy of potential capital intended for variable capital or contained in constant capital, which today belongs under the provisions of the "rule of law" only to the part of wage earners (higher tax brackets) who own it, has its sources in the past wage earners labor of many generations of wage earners in earlier times who, like today's wage earners, were denied participation in the distribution of the newly created monetary value or profit. Sixth, the profits of corporations and private owners of net cash balance or the return on capital from profits are used by higher taxpayers as the basis of corporate and private capital relations without which the modern capitalist or socialist community could not survive. Seventh, net cash profit in its final form is regularly located in private corporations of various profiles or privately owned by individuals who own or co-own corporations, bank capital, or any other capital that is fertilized by wage labor in the existing capital relation.

LESSONS FROM THE COVID19 VIRUS PANDEMIC

The fact that there is literally no partnership or moral obligation between the market wage earners of new value creators and the wage earners of corporate owners within democratic forms of political and social life, which is also a strong support for creative reproductive cycles and the harmonious existence of the entire modern American society is also indicated by the corona virus pandemic that spread to the whole world at the beginning of 2020 and is still going on, especially in the USA. What needs to be pointed out is that shortly after the time when the reasons for the long-term development of the coronavirus pandemic and its control were established, threatening a large number of victims among the active wage earners population of lower tax brackets living in very densely populated urban and suburban areas, decision was also made by the Federal, state and local city authorities to terminate all activities except those necessary for the minimum primarily health, food and transport functions in the daily life of communes and their citizens. Duties of all citizens, including wage earners during the pandemic in the USA were primarily kept to a minimum outside their apartments or family homes to prevent the transmission of the coronavirus from person to person, thus trying to control this extremely deadly viral infection in its upward trend by controlling the 15-20 days incubation period. In the months of January, February, March, April, May, June, July, and August 2020, this affected the entire American Federation especially the state and city of New York and south state. This decision to stop working most wage earners in all corporations, whether small or large, also meant s off and shutting down a huge number of wage earners across the United States (but also in other countries around the world), especially in industrial centers and megalopolises such as New York, Los Angeles, Chicago and other industrial centers and cities. More than 30,000,000 million (30-40-50 million according to various statistics ????) registered wage earners have been fired and referred to employment bureaus and agencies in charge of temporary unemployment benefits for unemployed wage earners, provided by the US Department of Labor. If we add to this population of wage earners at least 10 million unregistered able-bodied wage earning immigrants living and working in the USA, we can see a wage population of 40 million people who were left overnight and not voluntarily without the existential minimum they provided with their checks. If we add family members to this population, which means at least two or three more family people, this indicates a population whose number rises to numbers above 100,000,000 million USA residents who are victims of this pandemic. There are almost no indications that the pandemic was created by the capitalist or socialist capital relations typical of the economic crises and cataclysms of 1933, 2008, and in the legal everyday life of modern humanity these two dominant sociopolitical systems cannot be blamed for the world's viral suffering. What they can be accused of is that they met the pandemic completely unprepared and in confusing relations. The course itself and the consequences of the pandemic, however, point to the extreme weaknesses of these dominant socio-economic systems, especially in their global appearances around the world, which in this case and the tragic mass scale of the pandemic within social life manifest themselves uncontrollably, especially among lower-class wage earners who have almost no savings or cash reserves with which to temporarily support their families, unlike upper-tax wage earners or owners of dominant capital who can secure this for themselves. With the cessation of work due to the coronavirus pandemic, no wage earner received a severance pay or a guarantee that the corporation in which he worked until yesterday would bear his expenses in the amount of his regular check during the pandemic. The reason for this is the fact that indicates that the employer has no such obligations directly to its wage earners. In addition, the employer is not obliged to form funds for that purpose, and corporations simply do not have them. The money provided by the US Department of Labor that will go to unemployed wage earners if they report to the Department of Labor's agencies, which distribute financial aid in their province, belongs to the wage earners population, its corporation and other tax money paid to federal funds in the earlier tax period. Unfortunately, these benefits are never equal to the regular previous earnings that the wage earner earned through his current work, but are significantly lower and are subject to tax liabilities of about 30% on average, which indicates that if your fee is $ 600 per week for payment, approximately $ 400 dollars per week remain after tax deduction, and this amount enters the sum of your annual income at the end of the year which is also taxed. In relation to the costs incurred by the average American family with one or two children, this amount is completely insufficient to the needs and the "basket"(CPI) that indicates a tolerant standard of living and costs during a the covid19 virus pandemic. Catastrophic consequences, apart from wage earners and their families in a chain reaction, occur in the entire social community. This is especially evident in local city and state institutions that are funded and in function by tax money. What is evident in this pandemic crisis that has forced both wage-earning capital owners and wage earners who are mere market wage-earners to stop working is the fact that without ongoing wage labor that secures the income of all social reproduction, economic cycles and social reproduction as a whole are completely paralyzed. The lessons offered from this forced creative abstinence can be summarized in a few sentences. In a time of abstinence and the forced cessation of work of American wage earners of all tax brackets, not a single cent of new value or use or turnover will be created in corporations whose wage earners do not work. No matter how much capital through stimulus funds (2.3 trillion) the federation has invested in rebuilding the working capacity of US corporations and no matter how much

capital is owned by wage earners owning capital in corporations or financial institutions and society in general,
that capital loses all function and fertilization without total current creative and self-creative wage earners labor
and wage earners labor of newly created value which is
transformed into turnover value with which after its realization in sale or in some other way we element new social
reproductions.

The shock and fear of catastrophic consequences throughout society is quite high (there are almost no previous
experiences of such catastrophic proportions) and still uncontrollable. In these circumstances, a parallel uncritical
floating awareness of extreme political beliefs is regularly formed among top government officials representing
the interests of dominant capital, primarily marked by
panicked decisions to reopen despite warnings from epi-
demiologists and medical teams about the possibility of an
even greater health catastrophe. The dictates of capital that
unconditionally mobilize the work of wage earners of all
tax brackets are constantly present in our consciousness
as a dominant solution, unfortunately very often without
moral obligation and consideration for the victims.

The return of wage earners to corporations where they
worked in the USA until before the pandemic crisis
caused by the coronavirus is based on new loans from
funds approved by both the Congress and the Senate of
the American Federation. The money will be provided by
the US Federal Reserve (a private institution authorized

to control financial and monetary institutions and markets) with newly printed amounts of cheap credit money that will be placed through low-interest loans that will be delivered to corporations through local banks at their request, according to the needs these corporations express. Repayments and "alimenting financing" and of new debt in both principal and interest of the corporation will be guaranteed by presenting its values from the past and new wage current work of future periods. The stimulus package of money from the Congress of the Senate and the US government intended for the revitalization of corporate business is from the total amount of 2.3 trillion dollars, intended for 560 billion non-refundable money to all citizens, but this amount is also intended for wage earners who are out of work for as long as the epidemic lasts, 500 billion is intended for lending to the reconstruction of large corporations, 377 billion is intended for smaller corporations, 339 billion is intended for states and local government, 155.5 billion for health care and 43.7 billion for education. In the entire approach to the revitalization of the re-production process, in addition to these sums provided by the decision of US Senate, Congress, Government, and the US Federal Reserve institutions we do not see the personal money of owners and co-owners of corporations and corporate capital nor is it being discussed at the moment, and it is not known at this time what the sums from private capital and reserve corporate funds intended for the revitalization of US corporations are and if they are already in circulation or prepared to be used in addition to US Federal Reserve loans.

Both the US Congress and the Senate believe that this is a fair distribution of the stimulating money of the Federal Reserve Institution intended primarily for economic and creative entities of corporations and wage earners. As the overall tragic consequences of the pandemic are unpredictable, it is almost inevitable that the Federal Reserve's stimulus funds will increase over time. The "too big to fail" platform is being used again ("business is too big to be allowed to go bankrupt"). Based on this platform, most of the incentive money is intended for either smaller or larger US corporations. It is important to note that this money is a new debt of the USA that can be repaid in the future only from the newly created value of wage earners current work of the future. Taxes and tax brackets of wage earners in future periods are likely to be a different burden. It is difficult to predict, but again, a significantly higher burden on corporate tax liabilities will also be necessary, as will the burden on the private wealth of US corporate owners to manage US debt in the future.

At the moment, the existing distribution of incentive money is especially suitable for wage earners that are owners of corporations of all types (production and trade of goods, banks and other corporations) from higher tax brackets who, regardless of their private capital or corporate reserve money (which they should not be used in addition to incentive money), ensure their future participation in the accumulation and profit money of their corporations which will be realized for their benefit by their wage earners with their future work and the stimulating capital available.

All other wage earners without capital cannot participate in the use of extremely favorable bank loans or have the privilege of someone else earning income for them.... It seems that 85% of US wage earners who are recognized as low-wage wage earners in the category without capital are again predetermined only for a non-refundable incentive or a reduced weekly wage compensation by the Ministry of Labor (Labor Department), which is not enough to cover the basic needs of the daily life of wage earners.

Literally all wage earners, not only those wage earners who are owners of capital and owners of corporations who with these status features and real ownership ensure control of capital relations and legal protection of their borrowings of cheap money, should get favorable loans according to their needs. When we say all, then we mean ordinary market wage earners and their needs for the revitalization of living conditions in which they can be, with the assistance of credit money, functional reproduction creators again. In the existing legal system, the wage-earner should have the same principled characteristics as any other capital. Acquiring the right to earmarked loans to consolidate their living and social standards at favorable interest rates (not just minimum one-time grants) which should also be backed by the US government, Congress and the Senate as a guarantor guaranteeing full employment of wage earners and thus their functional partnership ability to repay their loans. An essential and fundamental starting point for these loans, should be to ensure the earnings of all wage earners, both wage earning capital owners and market wage earners who are not capital owners, guaranteed by federal and local authorities in a coordinated relationship. The world economic power of the USA has this opportunity to organize future socio-economic reproductions in this way. The question that is open and inconsistent and the reason such decisions are not made in favor of market wage earners even in crisis situations is still an unanswered regarding to whom belongs the net monetary gain or profit of current wage creation in modern capitalist and socialist society. If the market wage earner is equated in all rights, including the right to net profit, with wage earners who own dominant capital, there would be an outflow of large sums of net profit (money) and capital in favor of market wage earners. The modern political legal and economic establishment of the USA, like many other countries of capitalist economic culture, although they know that the unfolding of the historical drama between wage earners and capital is inevitable, is not ready to make such concessions to their wage earners nor is there a force that could make them do it.

We would like to remind you that the entire quantitative and qualitative volume of USA money is in circulation, even the one that is yet to be printed for the needs of the US Federal Reserve Institution. There are no states, banks or financial institutions, trade and infrastructure and other institutions that create new value through their current work if this new value is not already created by productive creative work and is not based on current wage earners labor in the sphere of production of means of production or production of means of consumption. All banks, including the US Federal Reserve Institution, secure and accumulate their income or the income of their associated banks, usually through interest and principal repayment installments with which they have indebted the borrowings of operating banks. Operating banks draw and condition the collection of their debts from the current value of wage labor that is realized on the market through the turnover value, and is also reported as an available fee to loan-sharking banks for functional participation in the realization of the turnover value. From the newly created value of current wage earners labor, all other obligations of not only corporations and wage earners but also the whole society are financially alimented in fundamental functions, which we have already illustrated by describing the purpose of tax money at the federal state or local level. What has been orchestrated as before in mass economic crises on countless occasions, with printed money from the Federal Reserve Institution intended for the revitalization of American corporate business and taxpayers, due to the coronavirus pandemic has primarily ensured the growth of corporate capital (especially financial capital) and profits but also the profits of the wage earners who are owners and co-owners of the capital invested in those corporations. As before, in this case the emphasis is on lending to corporations and their owners. In addition to the credit function, the emphasis is on ensuring all vital functions of the capital relation dictated by the dominant capital. No measures have been observed by either the government or the US Senate or Congress to indicate the formation of pragmatic low-interest loans (or interest-free loans) for capital less wage earners in the lower tax brackets. There is no economic reason for all wage earners who do not own corporate capital to qualify for interest-free loans or borrowings that can solve their complex and difficult problems caused by coronavirus pandemic. In addition, this is found in the moral partnership code and the ratio of dominant capital to 85% of the market wage earners. Unfortunately, such loans intended for the wage population of lower tax brackets in the banking supply market do not exist, as they do not exist in the concept of the Federal Reserve. The concept of equivalent treatment of all wage earners and those who own capital and those who are market paid to be its creators (as well as the entire capital system) is absolutely inevitable in modern and future capitalist systems of the world. The needs of modern American citizens, especially families in crisis situations, are marked by enormous costs that, in their current seriousness, are no less important than the corporate costs for which Congress and the Senate are working to revitalize them. If we recall the illustration given in Attachment: 8 and 9, which indicates the expansion and increase of the capital layer based on the creative current work of wage earners within the spiral vortex, we must also ask what happens to the cohesion and balance of centripetal and centrifugal forces within the creative reproductive body of the spiral (socio-political communities) when going through cataclysms such as this pandemic caused by the coronavirus, which completely eliminated and stopped human wage labor. At these moments we emphasize the dominating centripetal force which tries to draw all the remaining values in the spiral vortex into the smallest possible radius of rotation and if it is not intervened by a suitable means primarily human creative work to re-form the wider radius of centrifugal force and re-expansion of the ellipse, the disaster of civilization ending up in a kind of "black hole" into which we are drawn by the centripetal force of the dialectical opposites of total spiral and universal motion seems inevitable. This deviation based on centrifugal force and the creation of a new increased dominant capital depends significantly and exclusively on creative current wage labor, of course in healthy and safe conditions for the creator. As mankind does not have the tools to resist quickly and effectively to epidemic of the virus which affects a population of 14-15 million people, it is difficult to imagine the reach and real threat of far more serious disasters that could be caused by reckless environmental human behavior that will be much larger. In the pandemic of coronavirus that disrupted health, especially the function of the lungs in the human body, and in connection with that, without oxygen, this basic and irreplaceable chemical element, over 14-15,000,000 (of which 300,000-400,000 thousands died) millions people around the world have suffered (4,000,000 million in the USA). (Statistic in June 2020) Unlike in viral pandemic, in environmental disasters, if we do not change the uncontrolled global and forced dictates of the oxygen-deprived victim capital and other basic living conditions like the coronavirus pandemic, we could face far greater and more devastating consequences.

In modern capitalist society and modern socialism of the world, natural cataclysms as well as economic crises of various causes and consequences create a whole series of very visible lessons and indicators that point to the catastrophic weaknesses of modern capital relations between capitalist and socialist communities. However, it seems that the whole of humanity, as well as its most developed parts, has not yet reached the necessary creative maturity that could change our existing creative and self-creative reality, subordinated to the dictates of capital.

DOMINANT CAPITAL DICTATORSHIP

How to understand the perfect dictate of dominant capital in the USA today? If we remember 2019, American economic and social reproduction generated GDP of 21.220 trillion dollars. It is planned to realize 22,111 trillion dollars in 2020 and 24,000 trillion dollars in 2024. This plan is also a sequence of dictates of total US capital over several years that defines us in our daily social life and work, but also in relation to other economies of the world which we want to (and must) dominate according to the nature of capital. Using modern legal organization (rule of law), upper-class taxpayers who are both owners of dominant capital and also owners of 8-hour (and much higher) value of current work of the largest part of the wage population conditioned by the growth of universal, particular and singular capital, govern the entire community, the next legal dictate of capital and capital relations that characterizes the daily creative life and practice of communities both within the United States and abroad as far as creative reach that begins with American capital goes. To clarify this, although all wage earners participate in the implementation of the plan of social and economic reproductions imposed by dictates on a given amount of dominant capital, the real planners (dictators) on whom the participation of most wage earners depends are exclusively wage earners who own dominant capital. The rest of the wage earners (dictated or conditional wage earners) from the lower tax brackets (85% of the wage earner population) represent the means (expenditure) of realizing the dictates of dominant capital, in fact the wage plan of capital owners, as well as all democratic bodies of local, state or federal dominant capital. The 22.111 trillion dollars given to us in 2020 in "our economic plans" is a fundamental direct determinant that forms our creative consciousness which, according to our status wage characteristics, knows no other means of its survival, except those modern tools and means that help us realize dictatorship of capital in order to reach or exceed the sum of the given GDP, and it could not be concluded that the conditions for the abolition of the dictatorship of capital in modern civilizational history exist, neither in the USA nor in other less developed parts of world economic systems. Previous experiences indicate that no economic catastrophe, nor the modern health catastrophe caused by coronavirus pandemic that affects the whole world and threatens massive loss of human wage lives does not change the rules of organization of either capitalist or socialist communities and their capital relations. The dictates of the fertilization of capital and its growth do not see their victims no matter how many of them are there.

Generations of human beings are disappearing from the historical scene, leaving behind for millennia an open question to which there is still no complete answer. "In our wage-earning social and individual life in the present and future creative millennia, in the absence of a different practice of accepting our human being in the creative horizons of current work, are we really predestined, without resistance as a being, to be consciously subordinated to the dominant dictates of capital and existing practice of capital relations?"

A complete answer to this question exists neither as a practice nor as a vision of the most imaginative creators. However, both quantitative and qualitative change in higher levels of creativity and self-creativity in and out of the human being is constantly formed from his overall absolutely independent creative current human work, which regularly achieves its absolute independence based primarily on the universal movement, even in the worst slavery practice.

Dominant capital, which in its origin is the past creative work of wage earners, cannot survive without a symbiosis with wage labor. In order for this symbiosis to be complete and based on moral universal principles, the creative wage labor of the future will primarily have to create the processes and rule of law of all wage earners involved in the process of creating and marketing the realized new values within social reproductions in order to participate in the distribution of the final social profit and the realized monetary gain for their personal benefit. In this way, enormous creative motives and energy of wage earners of all strata and owners of capital and non-owner wage earners will be released and new more rational conditions of creativity will be established for all wage earners of social communities without conditioned dictates of dominant capital. Dominant capital in the new conditions will grow into capital that obliges us to personal creative participation through current creative work in social and economic reproductions in which new value will be realized, but also equal right to personal income and distribution of final social and corporate profit according to labor contribution of individual wage earners or total wage earning layers. The right to share the net social profit or profit of all wage earners will be based in the future on the abolition of the legal maxim which for now defines the use and turnover value of wage labor in the 8th hour work in favor of the wage-earning capital owners, except for the part guaranteed to the wage earner (wage) as a value that unconditionally belongs to the owners of dominant capital, regardless of its scope. This legal form of the basic provisions of modern capital relations and capitalism and socialism, which is based on the maxim, will be constantly the subject of criticism, and also the subject of creative changes in the wage-earning population of the future.

The subject of the entire human history, as well as the subject of modern and future human communities, will continue to be the overall creative current wage labor, regardless of whether the protagonist of the current labor is the wage earner who is the owner of the dominant capital or not. All other models and theories are going to be more and more out of needed focus.

BORO STIPANOVIĆ
Biography thru WORK EXPERIENCE AND EMPLOYMENT IN

NEW YORK: 1990-2020 (present day)

1990 – 1995. Philippe Farley Gallery. Fine Art Restorer.
Restoration of fine art, antique furniture, particularly French 17th and 18th century pieces in one of the leading antique dealers in New York at the time. Gilding, gold leafing. Conservation of art.

1995 - 1997 REMCO New York. Founder and head of the Wood Restoration Department.
Maintenance and preservation company. Worked on various exteriors and interiors including the 79th Street synagogue at 2nd Avenue, the Argentinean Embassy, Greenwood Cemetery Church (Brooklyn), The Frick Collection,

1997 – 2009 - Metropolitan Club. House Decorative Artist and Restorer of interiors.
Maintenance, restoration and conservation of the interiors and the exterior of the 19th century Stamford White National Landmark Building. Extensive gilding and wood restoration projects. Restoration of massive decorative objects such as chandelier, doors, ceilings, stucco, carvings, and campo decorations.

OTHERE EXPIRIENCE And EMPLOIMENTS before 1990 in Croatia where I start working as follow:

1973- 1976. Philosophy and sociology professor." Eugen Kumicic" and "Branko Semelić" Lyceum. Pula, Croatia
High School level philosophy classes for junior and senior students.

1976 – 1980. Philosophy professor and director of. "Jurica Kalc" CommunitCollege. Pula, Croatia.
Dean of Faculty. Responsibilities included faculty development and mentoring, as well as management of current programs. Teaching adult education courses.

1980 – 1984. Urban Development Sociologist. City Urban Development Agency of Pula, Croatia.
Investigation of demographic movements, land use policy and regulations, programming, urbanization rezoning and housing developments... Research of cultural landmarks and monuments.

1984- 1987. Cultural Consultant of Education and Culture of Municipality of Pula, Croatia.
Verification and development of educational and cultural programs. Coordination of municipal resources, institutions, and staff in preservation of cultural heritage, and utilization of appropriate preservation techniques.

1987 – 1990. Executive Director. Scientific Research Library of University of Pula/University V. Bakarić, Rijeka, Croatia. Initialized the creation of library's computerization and integration into world research systems. Creation of an extensive Art collection. Cataloging, exhibiting and preservation of antique books collection. Acquisition of personal/memorial collections from several prominent writers, artists, and composers.

1998 – 1998 Editor. Cultural Journal "Istra".
Member of the executive editorial board, working effectively with publishing professionals, editing manuscripts, and coordinating the publishing of contemporary cultural research and writing.

EDUCATION:
1969 – 1973.   BA Philosophy and BA Sociology, Faculty of Philosophy, University of Zagreb.

1985 - 1992. Restoration and Conservation Course in Europe, Italy, and Community College NY

OTHER PROFESSIONAL EXPERIENCE:
2006 – 2008. Iolani Palace Collections Honolulu Hawaii. Restoration and preservation consultant and restorer **Restoration** work on several art objects from the Hawaiian Royal Collection as well as consulting on the preservation of this important national collection.
Conducted restoration workshops and demonstrations for the museum's patrons and donors. Assisted fundraising for future restoration programs.

1998 - 2002. Restoration Lectures and guided tours through Restoration projects at the Metropolitan Club New York for fine arts and art history college programs.

AWARDS:
2006. Pride of Place, Gilding Award:" Sepp Leaf Inc" New York. First place awarded for the Interior Commercial Gilding, "Presidents' Foyer-Metropolitan Club".
Project featured in several architectural and design magazines.

2012 Diploma of Hawaiian state preservation society for restoration of several art object of Iolani Palace Honolulu Hawaii.

AUTOR of 4 BOOKS: "Capital and dominant Capital relations", "Capital as the scourge of god", "Restorers Travelogue", "History as dictatorship of capital".

CPSIA information can be obtained
at www.ICGtesting.com
Printed in the USA
BVHW020723111020
590768BV00021B/771